Diss

MW01284460

"A New Beginning," or a Revised Past?

President Barack Obama's Cairo Speech

By Mary Grabar, Ph.D. & Brian Birdnow, Ph.D.

Dissident Prof Press

Dissident Prof Education Project, Inc.

P.O. Box 156

Scottdale, GA 30079

www.dissidentprof.com

For all the Dissident Professors, Students, and Supporters who resist the pressures to conform to the ideological demands of the day.

We would like to thank the following dissident professors for their help on this project:

Dr. Jim Dixey, Director of Graduate Business Career Services, Mays Business School, Texas A&M University; Dr. Timothy Furnish, Islamic world geopolitical analyst, consultant and author, and former professor of Islamic, African and World history; Dr. Martin Slann, Dean and Professor of Political Science, The University of Texas at Tyler; Dr. Tina Trent, independent scholar.

Dissident Prof Guide Books for Dissident Students — College, High School, and Lifelong Learners

About the Series: Editor: Mary Grabar, Ph.D.

Dissident Prof Guide Books are written by college professors for:

HIGH SCHOOL AND COLLEGE STUDENTS confronted with biased teachers, textbooks, and assignments. Our college professors offer information, analysis, and helpful bibliographies.

LIFELONG LEARNERS AND CITIZENS seeking to continue their educations and looking for a handy resource on topics that concern and interest them.

For both formal and informal study--we hope the Dissident Prof Guide Books lead to more reading and discussion.

TABLE OF CONTENTS

Chapter 1

Introduction: What this book is about

On June 4, 2009, President Barack Obama delivered a much-anticipated speech at Cairo University in Egypt. Coming on the heels of Obama's worldwide "Apology Tour," the speech signaled not only how Obama viewed his country, but how he would set himself apart in "a new beginning" that would change America's course from what he presented as a dangerous and belligerent approach by his predecessor, President George W. Bush. The version of history that Obama presented, however, cast the Middle East and Islam in a more favorable light than the facts would warrant.

The President's Cairo Speech carries great historical and political significance because it set out Obama's Middle East policy and his vision of the United States in the international arena. It also presents insights into the character of the president. Like George Washington's Farewell Address and John F. Kennedy's Inauguration Speech, the Cairo Speech will likely be studied as an important document in American history.

Obama's promise of "a new beginning" cannot yet be evaluated critically. Unfolding events--and the outcome of the promises made--will determine the greatness of the speech. This happens only in retrospect, with the benefit of historical reflection.

The Cairo Speech, however, is already being reprinted in anthologies and textbooks, and is taught to students as a hallmark of rhetorical brilliance and as an unalloyed diplomatic victory. The cult of personality that has sprung up around President Obama is carried into classrooms where educators "teaching the speech" encourage students to unquestioningly accept the President's calls for action and support. Such directives stand opposite to American traditions and ideals of independent thinking and self-government, as well as to standards of excellence in scholarship.

This Dissident Prof Guide offers resources for students who are being asked to admire, not analyze, Obama's Cairo Speech. The Guide includes a handy point-by-point analysis of the speech, a bibliography of trusted historical sources, and an account of the numerous errors of historical fact, including those pointed out by commentators and historians in the days following the speech's delivery. It will serve as a handy reference for all who might wish to understand and analyze this pivotal moment in our nation's history.

The Dissident Prof Guide includes:

- Summary of the purpose and strategies of political speeches, going back to Aristotle and Cicero
- Analysis of rhetorical strategies employed in this speech
- An overview of American foreign policy since the founding of the United States
- Comparisons to other speeches by Presidents Lincoln, Kennedy, and Reagan
- A summary of the reactions to the speech by historians, political commentators, and American Muslims
- Information about events in the Middle East since the speech was delivered
- Strategies for dealing with biased assignments

Introduction: Who We Are

Mary Grabar earned her Ph.D. in English from the University of Georgia in 2002. She has written extensively on education, politics, and American culture for such publications as *Townhall, PJ Media, The Weekly Standard, Roll Call, Minding the Campus, Accuracy in Media,* and many others. She has written several reports on radicalism in education and participated in several conferences sponsored by America's Survival. She appears frequently on radio and television to discuss issues in education. In 2011, she launched her non-profit, Dissident Prof Education Project, Inc., and writes for and edits the Dissident Prof website, www.dissidentprof.com. Mary is also a published poet and fiction writer, and currently teaches English at Emory University.

Brian Birdnow earned his Ph.D. in American History from St. Louis University in 2000. His book, *The St. Louis Five: The Smith Act, Communism and the Federal Courts in Missouri 1952-1958,* was published by the Edwin Mellen Press in 2005. His most recent book, *Gerald Ford: The All-American President* (Nova Science Foundation), was published in 2011. His other publications include six chapters in the *American Presidential Encyclopedia,* articles in the *Claremont Review* and *Townhall,* and reviews in *The Journal of American History.* He currently teaches as an adjunct professor of history at Lindenwood University and at Harris Stowe State University, both in Missouri.

Why and How This Book Came About

By Mary Grabar

Towards the end of the Fall 2011 semester I received in my campus mailbox what many professors do: a sample copy of a textbook from the publisher's sales rep. There is nothing remarkable about this except that when I looked through the table of contents I noticed President Barack Obama's "A New Beginning" speech, commonly known also as the "Cairo Speech" because of its locale of delivery, Cairo University. The "new beginning" was intended to reference a new attitude toward the Muslim world.

As I noted in my *Minding the Campus* article, "The Terrible Textbooks of Freshman Comp," Obama's Cairo speech was positioned amidst a selection of essays heavily weighted towards a liberal, progressive, and even socialist, perspective.[1]

In my freshman composition classes at Emory University where I was teaching, as well as at other colleges where I have taught in the past, I have used presidential speeches as recordings of historical and political moments, and as examples of classical rhetoric. But these speeches had been limited to presidents whose records were known. All of them—George Washington, Abraham Lincoln, Woodrow Wilson, Ronald Reagan—were part of the historical record. Having withstood the test of time, their speeches had become part of the rhetorical canon.

But here was a speech, published in a collection soon after the president had taken office, and who would run for reelection. Most college students are old enough to vote, so, in a sense, the inclusion of Obama's words could be taken as a kind of professor-approved campaign literature.

I wondered then how many other textbooks included Obama's speeches and written works. To my shock, most did. Some included them in volumes that came out while he was still campaigning for president. It struck me as a clear violation of ethical principles to teach a candidate's writings during a time of election, especially with the uncritical, laudatory prose that the textbook editors had placed around it. After all, no one knew the outcome of Obama's presidency, even as his speeches were heralded to students.

But such inclusion in curricular materials matched what I observed among my colleagues. When I still taught there, I'd walk past classrooms at Georgia Perimeter College and hear Obama's speeches played for students. Professors took entire classes to watch his inauguration in the assembly hall. They had Obama-Biden campaign material tacked up on the doors of their offices.

The uncritical campaigning for Obama was incorporated into K-12 education too. Elementary school children sang songs in praise of Obama, during his campaign and shortly after taking office.[2] Teenage boys marched in military formation while shouting out "yes, we can, take responsibility for our own lives."[3] They credited Obama by marching forward from their line formations, exclaiming, "Because of Obama, I aspire to be. . ." a lawyer, architect, and similar professions. They then listed the features of Obama's health care plan as if they had each memorized a point from campaign literature.[4] High school teachers gave students credit for working on his first campaign. During his second campaign, one teacher in Virginia asked his eighth-grade honors class to do opposition research on Republican candidates, prepare a strategy paper, and locate an individual in the Obama campaign to whom the paper could be sent.[5] Textbooks featured him. The eighth-grade McDougal Littell Literature textbook, published in 2008, had a 15-page spread on Obama.[6] At the beginning of the 2009 school year, in an unprecedented and highly controversial White House effort, Obama's address to schoolchildren was beamed into classrooms across the country, accompanied by special curriculum materials.[7]

It's not that college students needed encouragement during the 2008 campaign. They were already coming to my classes dressed in t-shirts with larger-than-life images of the upturned profile of the presidential candidate, often with glittery lettering and his trademarked symbol of a road adapted from the American flag, which went with the newly designed Presidential seal that was used between the election and inauguration. Obama had energized the youth vote with optimistic messages of "hope and change," sending more young voters to the polls than in previous elections, and widening the gap between them and older voters.[8] While the percentage of white voters pulling the Democrat lever remained consistent from recent presidential elections, the percentage of minority and young (18-29) voters jumped, giving Obama his winning edge.

I had not seen such a phenomenon of political celebrity, and I remembered presidential elections going back to the 1960s. Sure, I had seen college students sporting bumper stickers for the candidate of their choice or a t-shirt with a campaign slogan, but I had never seen the visage of a candidate plastered over young bodies before. Certainly, there were none of George W. Bush; nor were there any of Al Gore or John Kerry.

To someone who immigrated to this country from what was Communist Yugoslavia as a very young child this was a disturbing development. The fact that our nation was a "nation of laws," and not of men, set it apart from Communist Yugoslavia. The Founding Fathers warned about potential dangers of charismatic leaders and set up a system of government so that national identity would not be synonymous with a particular personality. Presidents accordingly had displayed respect for their roles as citizen leaders, as of the people, beholden to the Constitution and expecting respect granted to the office rather than the person.

But this had changed. Educators were in on the act. Schools were named after the newly elected president. Music teachers were leading children in newly composed songs to Obama, with lyrics that proclaimed devotion and support. Young boys marched in military formation and chanted promises to follow the example of Obama.

Professors were presenting conference papers uncritically heralding Obama's policies and rhetorical prowess, while, as usual, making digs at George W. Bush[9] (as they had during his presidency). I got a taste of the lingering contempt for Bush and conservatives while attending the annual meeting of the Conference on College Composition and Communication in April 2011; I then reported on it for *Minding the Campus*.[10] In April 2012, I learned about a Harvard University course called "Understanding Obama" to be taught by a longtime supporter of Obama, Charles Ogletree, in the spring semester 2013.[11]

Ogletree, a radical, became Obama's mentor when he met him at Harvard in 1988. As a student, Ogletree edited a campus Black Panther newspaper and traveled to Africa and Cuba with student activist groups. He continued such activism[12] as a professor by joining groups demanding reparations for descendents of black slaves and denouncing investigations of former Black Panther members for their role in the 1971 killing of a policeman.[13]

The Obama Harvard course promises to focus on such academically suspect angles as Obama's "views as a biracial child" and "on the way in which race, religion, and politics have impacted the development of President Obama as a leader." Interestingly, the course description assumes Obama's continued presidency in 2013, his second term, with the promise (in 2013) to analyze "the challenges he faces as President of the United States in establishing both his domestic and global policies."[14]

This is not the first time Obama's name has come up in the college catalogue. Other courses, in Government and English, at Harvard presented Obama as a touchstone for course content and mentioned him by name in descriptions.

Harvard is not alone. For fall semester 2012, freshmen at Emory University can fulfill freshman composition requirements by enrolling in ENG 101: "Barack Obama's Fighting Words: Interpreting Rhetoric in Historical Contexts." The course promises to focus on Obama's "most important speeches between his 2008 and 2012 presidential bids" and to compare them to speeches of "other historically significant figures," like Abraham Lincoln, Booker T. Washington, W.E.B. Du Bois, Rev. Dr. Martin Luther King, Jr., Rev. Jeremiah Wright, and Hillary R. Clinton. Required "textbooks" include Obama's two autobiographies and a collection of his speeches, titled *Words That Changed a Nation: The Most Celebrated and Influential Speeches of Barack Obama* and *Power in Words: The Stories behind Barack Obama's Speeches from the State House to the White House.*

Other universities had already been offering courses on Obama's rhetoric. In the spring of 2010, the University of Kansas, Lawrence, offered ENGL 340, "Barack Obama and the African American Rhetorical Tradition." But these are only some of the ones that show up in a casual search. Most universities do not make descriptions of course offerings available to the public. This is not to mention the numerous lectures and debates about Obama on our campuses—almost all expounding on the historical significance, in a positive sense, of his election.

In addition to the inappropriateness of focusing on one person, most of the educational efforts on behalf of Barack Obama have been short on criticism and long on praise. None seem to extend from an objective, scholarly perspective. This is what I found when I examined the introductory and explanatory material accompanying the Obama selections in various textbooks.

I also noticed that in spite of the plethora of criticism in the media and by history professors about the historical inaccuracies in the speech, none were pointed out in the textbook. In fact, the editors simply let the fallacies stand, and even enhanced their intended persuasiveness with supportive footnotes! I noticed rhetorical strategies and logical fallacies not pointed out, ironically, in a composition textbook. I felt there should be a way to inform students and lead them to other sources. Obviously, most teachers who would teach this speech out of this textbook would not provide alternatives. This Dissident Prof Guide is intended to fill in the gap.

Tips for the Student:

This is intended to be a guide only and not intended to be included in your bibliography or Works Cited page. Do not quote without giving credit to the original source, which we strongly encourage you to read for yourself. So, read this guide to get an overall perspective. Go to the original sources cited here. Find out more on your own. Consider the other side to make yourself a stronger debater. If you disagree with the points in the speech, find a source that agrees and then explain why that source is wrong. Back up your points with facts and logic, and in a manner that demonstrates that you have considered all angles.

If you do all these things and hand in a well-written paper, it will be much more difficult for a biased professor or teacher to give you a bad grade.

If you have any questions, send an email to studentquestions@dissidentprof.com. We'll get one or more of our professors to address your questions (though we will not proofread papers).

Chapter 2

The Reception to "A New Beginning": How Scholars and Commentators Reacted to the Speech:

CBS News, hardly a conservative organ, reported that praise for "A New Beginning" usually focused on its "delivery," but noted that even the *Huffington Post* marked the "lack of substance in the words." William Bradley's column there claimed that the speech's arena itself was reason for its success: "The positions [Obama] laid out are positions he had in his campaign. But he did say it all at once, and quite well. In that sense, to borrow a phrase from Marshall McLuhan, the medium is the message." Of course, once the speech is put into a textbook it loses the benefit of the "medium."[15]

Other, partisan organs predictably praised the speech and did not address the accuracy of the historical references. The *Guardian* in Britain rhapsodized, calling it "a speech which encompassed not only contemporary conflicts but past ones; a speech which would not only restate common values but redefine them in terms of Islamic teaching and the Qur'an." The editors claimed that Obama "succeeded spectacularly," and "given the mine-strewn nature of the terrain on which he was venturing," he "displayed a mastery of touch."

Furthermore, according to the *Guardian*, "[Obama] achieved his aims without side-stepping key issues or keeping to the safety of rhetorical high ground." Although Guardian editors caution that action is needed to back up words, they devoted most of the editorial to praise of the evenhandedness and historical accuracy of the speech: Obama "summon[ed] the full forces of his biography, the civil rights movement and South Africa. . . ."

According to them, the new president masterfully ("in plain, unequivocal language") simultaneously condemned the Holocaust and "acknowledged 60 years of Palestinian dislocation, the daily humiliation of occupation, and described the current situation for Palestinians as intolerable."[16]

The *New York Times* editorial board focused less on the rhetoric and more on the comparison to George W. Bush, setting up their analysis by claiming that when Bush "spoke in the months and years after Sept. 11, 2001, we often — chillingly — felt as if we didn't recognize the United States." It was after listening to Obama that they "recognized the United States" — a country not like Bush's "racked with fear and bent on vengeance."

Obama spoke "unwaveringly" and "unequivocally," while doing a masterful political balancing act between the Muslim and non-Muslim world. The charges that Obama had been apologizing for the United States, on an "apology tour," the *New York Times* editorial board called a "gross misreading."[17]

Obama's critics, however, pointed to a number of instances where he did seem to apologize. Among these are the following, compiled from the Heritage Foundation:[18]

1. Strasbourg, France, April 3, 2009: President Obama confessed that America "has shown arrogance and been dismissive, even derisive" toward Europe and failed to appreciate Europe's leading role in the world. Most Americans consider the USA to have the leading role in the world.

2. Interview with *Al Arabiya* newspaper, January 27, 2009: The President confessed that "We have not been perfect" in our relations with the Islamic world. He said that we could restore the "respect and partnership that America had with the Muslim world...30 years ago." (In 1979 when Jimmy

Carter was President, Muslim revolutionaries, led by the Ayatollah Khomeini captured the U.S. embassy and held 52 Americans hostage for over a year; they were released minutes after the inauguration of Ronald Reagan in 1981.)

3. Port of Spain, Republic of Trinidad & Tobago, April 17, 2009: At the Summit of the Americas, Obama apologized for the fact that, "...we have at times been disengaged, and at times we sought to dictate our terms." He called his own term "...a new chapter of engagement..."

4. G-20 Summit, London, United Kingdom, April 2, 2009: Here the President said that he had brought about "...some restoration of America's standing in the world." He went on to say that we needed "...to forge partnerships as opposed to simply dictating solutions." Obama signaled a new kind of diplomacy, cast as different from the one of the simpler times of the World War II era: "Well if there's just Roosevelt and Churchill sitting in a room with a brandy, that's an easier negotiation. But that's not the world we live in, and it shouldn't be the world that we live in."

5. The National Archives, Washington D.C., May 21, 2009: In this speech Obama accused his predecessor of lying, stating, "all too often our government trimmed facts and evidence to fit ideological predispositions." Obama claimed that "all too often our government made decisions based on fear, rather than foresight." He finished by stating that, in the War on Terror, "We went off course."

6. G-20 Summit, London, united Kingdom, April 3, 2009: When asked if he believed in the concept of American exceptionalism Obama answered that he believed in this concept, "the same way that Brits believe in British exceptionalism, and the Greeks in Greek exceptionalism."

7. Speech to the Turkish Parliament, Ankara, Turkey, April 6, 2009: In this speech Obama stated, "The United States is still working through some of our own darker periods in our history. Facing the Washington Monument that I spoke of is a

memorial of Abraham Lincoln, the man who freed those who were enslaved even after Washington led our Revolution. Our country still struggles with the legacies of slavery and segregation, the past treatment of Native Americans." Critics found this negative and one-sided presentation of American history particularly insulting because it was made on foreign soil. Likewise, Obama made no mention of the help of the U.S. in preserving Turkey's independence in the face of provocative Soviet moves in 1946-49.

8. In a widely distributed opinion piece, "Choosing A Better Future In The Americas," on April 16, 2009, Obama positioned himself as a bold leader, initiating an unprecedented policy: "My Administration is committed to a new day. We will renew and sustain a broader partnership between the United States and the hemisphere on behalf of our common prosperity and our common security." He did not mention Franklin D. Roosevelt's "The Good Neighbor Policy" or Ronald Reagan's "Caribbean Basin Initiative."

9. At the CIA Headquarters, in Langley, Virginia, on April 20, 2009, President Obama said, "Don't be discouraged that we have to acknowledge potentially we've made some mistakes."

10. During a speech at the National Archives in Washington, D.C., on May 21, 2009, Obama said, "Rather than keeping us safer, the prison at Guantanamo has weakened American national security. It is a rallying cry for our enemies." (Closing the Guantanamo base where terrorists are imprisoned was one of Obama's campaign promises. For various reasons, like national security, inability to find domestic space, and public opinion, Gitmo, as of this printing over three years after the speech, is still open.)

The *Times* editors, comparing Obama's six-month presidency to Bush's two terms, concluded, "After eight years of arrogance and bullying that has turned even close friends against the United States, it takes a strong president to acknowledge the mistakes of the past."[19]

The conservative *Washington Times*, in contrast, claimed "Obama gives a Bush speech," as their headline announced. They began by stating, "President Obama sounded like he was channeling President George W. Bush," and continued, "Much of the substance of Mr. Obama's address, titled 'A New Beginning' sounded like the same old song. One could easily remove the biographical references, redact a few of the sentences that are clearly critical of specific Bush administration policies, and pass it off as old Republican talking points."

They drew parallels to Bush's speeches on September 17, 2001; June 24, 2002; and May 18, 2008. These were but a few, they stated, with "many more, especially dealing with democratization, women's issues, religious freedom and the war in Afghanistan." In fact, Obama's pledge to "'confront violent extremism in all its forms' might as well have been taken from former Vice President Dick Cheney's briefcase."[20]

National Review editors similarly claimed that Obama's "defense of democracy as a universal form of government was closer to the Bush policy than anything Secretary of State Clinton has said recently."[21] In contrast to the *New York Times'* oft-repeated characterization of Bush as bellicose, the *Washington Times* editors pointed out, "We fully expected to hear something along the lines of what Mr. Bush said on Sept. 17, 2001: 'the face of terror is not the true faith of Islam...Islam is peace.'" They expressed surprise at the lack of reference to Islam as a "religion of peace," but noted "praise of the Muslim world for various (and debatable) historical accomplishments." Among these was a "historically mangled reference to Andalusia and Cordoba during the Spanish Inquisition" as evidence of Islam's "'proud tradition of tolerance.'" They pointed out that "both are sites of major Muslim massacres of Jews in the 11th century."[22]

Obama's attempt to elevate Islam garnered criticism from some American Muslims, as well. Kemal Silay, Stephen Schwartz, Irfan Al-Alawi, and Salim Mansur, of the Center for

Islamic Pluralism, in an editorial published by the Hudson Institute in New York took issue with historical inaccuracies in the speech, all done in the attempt, they felt, to pander to Muslims. They began by chastising Obama for boasting about his Muslim heritage for political purposes, by noting that as candidate he distanced himself from the religion. Echoing the *Washington Times*, they state that his speech "offered nothing new." They note, however, that the speech included "a number of erroneous and superficial notes."

Among these was "the patronizing habit of addressing Muslims with Islamic greetings, citations, and blessings." For non-Muslims to do this is "gratuitous and pretentious, and appears bizarre," as strange as a Muslim saying, "'Jesus is Lord.'" They also take him to task for denying divergences between Islam and Judaism and Christianity. After pointing out seven historical inaccuracies, they conclude that "Sloppy formulations and flattering oratory will not improve the condition of Muslims or non-Muslims." Clearly, these Muslims felt patronized by a politician. They did not view his speech as "a significant contribution to dialogue between Muslims and non-Muslims."[23]

The editors of *National Review* begin by noting the political nature of Obama's speech:

> A U.S. president addressing the world is in a very different situation from that of a religious leader interpreting a doctrine or a philosopher clarifying a logical argument. He is concerned principally not with the truth of his propositions but with their likely effects. That does not mean he can tell outright lies — they would be detected and he discredited — but it does suggest that he will stress some truths more than others and soften the harsher ones. And he will be right to do so if the effect is to reconcile civilizations and religions at risk of conflict with each other.

It is in this light that "A New Beginning" should be analyzed. For this, we need to go back to Aristotle, who "wrote the book" on rhetoric. Among his many lasting insights was that rhetoric has different purposes for different occasions. Included are political purposes.

Chapter 3

The Rhetorical Analysis

The forward thrust—the desire to direct future actions--is part of what makes such a speech political, as Aristotle explains in *The Rhetoric*. To make a fair analysis, one should note the occasion and purpose of the speech, and for "A New Beginning," it was to "reconcile civilizations." The other two types of speeches, according to Aristotle, as we may recall, are forensic (determining what happened in the past) and epideictic or celebratory (in praise or blame and dealing with the present).

The *National Review* editors are, in essence, echoing Aristotle in their rhetorical analysis and acknowledging Aristotle's definition of rhetoric as the art of persuasion. Aristotle rescued the bad reputation that rhetoric had acquired from the sophists, teachers for hire who taught young men how to use sleight-of-word to win cases in court. Aristotle, in launching his work with the claim, "Rhetoric is the counterpart of dialectic," put forth the idea that rhetoric can be used for good purposes.

Although they do not mention him by name, the editors are referring to the commonplaces as described by Aristotle. Once rhetoric is assigned the role of assisting dialectic—the search for truth through philosophical means—the duty for rhetoric becomes that of promoting what is true. Rhetoric aids in disseminating truth by reaching an audience not capable of the strict syllogistic reasoning of dialectic, as dramatized in Socrates' dialogues.

Once Aristotle has rescued the reputation of rhetoric, others, like the Roman statesman Cicero, assert its noble and useful function. Since the classical era, one caveat has accompanied each defense of rhetoric: that it promote the truth. Cicero, in his introduction to *De Oratore* ("On the Character of the Orator"), echoes the Greeks, like Isocrates and Aristotle, by stating, "'wisdom without eloquence does too little for the good of the states, but that eloquence without wisdom is generally highly disadvantageous and is never helpful.'"[24] He continues defining the character of an orator, and claims that "A knowledge of a vast number of things is necessary, without which volubility of words is empty and ridiculous."

Along with an understanding of the emotions and the "allaying or exciting the feelings of those who listen," must be "a certain portion of grace and wit, learning worthy of a well-bred man, and quickness and brevity in replying as well as attacking, accompanied with a refined decorum and urbanity."

In other words, underneath the fancy words must be knowledge. Cicero asserts,

> In my opinion, indeed, no man can be an orator possessed of every praiseworthy accomplishment, unless he has attained the knowledge of everything important, and of all liberal arts, for his language must be ornate and copious from knowledge, since, unless there be beneath the surface matter understood and felt by the speaker, oratory becomes an empty and almost puerile flow of words.[25]

As the *National Review* editors point out, we expect politicians and leaders to emphasize some facts and downplay others in the pursuit of finding common ground and good will. But clearly a line is drawn between emphasis, and misrepresentations or lies. The editors claim that "outright lies" would be "detected and discredited."[26]

Indeed, a number of historians have disputed the statements of historical fact in Obama's speech. Political partisans have ignored them. Whether they are "outright lies" or simply the result of ignorance, is not at issue. The fact is that this much-heralded speech is peppered with historical omissions, distortions, and falsehoods. The role of scholars is to assert the truth, without regard to ideology, and to correct such errors, regardless of their origins. In other words, college professors who author books should be above political goals.

The fact remains that, in spite of the immediate rise of complaints by historians, this speech was uncritically reprinted in textbooks. When errors of fact are simply repeated without correction — especially to those still undergoing their educations — they take on an authority and become part of the historical record.

Above all, at Dissident Prof, we believe in high standards of scholarship. Whether repeated by a Democrat or Republican, or of anyone else with a political goal, historical errors must be challenged, especially when they are presented to students.

We hope the following analysis of Obama's "A New Beginning" speech will help correct the historical errors now circulating widely in classrooms. We hope that the analysis will give the student a better understanding of the historical significance of the speech, of the historical references made in the speech, as well as of the rhetorical strategies employed.

Chapter 4

"A New Beginning's" Place in History: A Comparison to Speeches by Presidents Washington, Lincoln, Kennedy, and Reagan

President Barrack Hussein Obama delivered an address at Cairo University entitled "A New Beginning" on June 4, 2009. The address, known commonly as the "Cairo Speech," redeemed Obama's 2008 campaign promise to attempt to improve US-Islamic relations by delivering a speech on the same subject from a major Muslim city in the early months of his presidency. This effort was widely praised by liberals and moderates in the Western world, but largely panned by conservatives who referred to it as simply another stop on the Obama "apology tour."

President Obama saw the speech as an opportunity to repair American relations with the Muslim world, which he considered necessary after the supposed damage to this delicate relationship during the Presidency of George W. Bush, and the Republican call for a war on Islamic terrorism. The speech would serve to assure Muslims that America meant them no harm and was consistent with Obama's oft-repeated phrase that "America is not at war with Islam."

In addition to Obama's outreach to the Muslim world there were other factors in play. Obama often spoke privately about his personal experiences with Islam, and the realization that Islam and Christendom share common ideals such as monotheism and the joys of communitarian worship and family life. The President also sought, through the speech, to establish his credibility as a thoughtful and polished foreign policy intellectual who tried to create a state of true peace among equals, as opposed to the reckless and bellicose approach of his predecessor, George W. Bush. Some observers trace Obama's Nobel Peace Prize of October, 2009, to the Cairo Speech. They felt that the speech alone convinced the judges to award him the Nobel Peace Prize.

Historically speaking, Presidential speeches run the gamut from the mundane to the magnificent and it is difficult to place Obama's Cairo address in the proper context. The speech was widely anticipated and, thus, it received wide media coverage. In this respect it would mirror George Washington's Farewell Address.[27] Washington, having decided to retire at the end of his second term as President, proposed a farewell address to the nation. He solicited ideas and suggestions from Alexander Hamilton, and used these to prepare a draft address.[28] The "speech" was not delivered in person (due largely to technological limitations) but was published in newspapers on September 19, 1796.

Washington's valedictory address to the nation is reasoned, sober, and judicious. It contains little in the way of soaring rhetoric, or idealism. Contrary to President Obama's calls to change, or "remake" the world, Washington congratulates his countrymen on what they have accomplished in the early years of the republic, but warns them that imprudence and careless statecraft might cause everything built in twenty years to quickly crumble, possibly reflecting Edmund Burke's maxim that revolution could topple overnight what it took centuries to build. Washington warned first against the harmful spirit of political partisanship he saw growing in the country. He argued that the US Constitution provided for a government of laws, not men, and superseded the ambitions of politicians and their respective factions, which became the organized political parties of later years. He reminded his fellow citizens that the common American culture (Religion, Customs, Habits, & Political Principles) united the country and proved complementary, not divisive. He deplored what he considered to be insidious efforts to divide the country and set region against region. President Obama, by contrast, referred to the US Constitution and his duties very sparingly in the Cairo speech.

Washington also stressed the wisdom of steering clear of foreign entanglements, involving the country in unnecessary quarrels. He was justly proud of having kept America out of the war raging in Europe at the time, despite pressure from various quarters to join in on one side or the other. While not arguing for "isolation" as has been supposed, Washington strongly supported free and open trade with all nations and even advocated "temporary alliances for extraordinary emergencies." As a realist, Washington flatly stated that the country must maintain a "respectable defensive posture, underwritten by suitable establishments of force." A prudent foreign policy, backed by respectable military force would, "in all probability enable us to bid defiance to any power on earth." Washington thus contended that America could pursue a policy of peace through strength and independence of action. In contrast to Obama's implication that American strength breeds arrogance and militarism, Washington argued that American strength was a necessary prerequisite for general peace.

Lastly, Washington, mindful of the ghastly events that had recently occurred in revolutionary France, dismissed the notion that America was a secular state.   He concluded by appealing to the sacred in stating that, "Religion and morality are indispensable supports." He believed that public spiritedness could not exist without a strong private morality, founded squarely in religion. Washington, unlike many modern public figures, could not conceive of a republic founded on anything other than a Christian morality and this is a notion at odds with the ecumenical tone of Obama's Cairo speech.

A second good point of comparison for the Obama Cairo speech would be Lincoln's Second Inaugural Address.[29] The speech, delivered on March 4, 1865, outlined Lincoln's general approach to the problem of rebuilding and reuniting the nation as the Civil War thundered toward a conclusive victory for the Union forces. Lincoln urged magnanimity in victory, and the Christian religious overtones in this generally somber address were quite strong. Lincoln pushed the nation to continue the struggle to the end, but also to extend, "malice toward none, with charity for all, with firmness in the right, as God gives us to see the right." Lincoln, like Washington, easily invoked God and asked for divine guidance.

In terms of soaring rhetoric and a call to remake the world the Cairo speech bears a strong similarity to President John F. Kennedy's inaugural address of January 20, 1961.[30] Kennedy aimed his speech squarely at American youth, claiming that the new generation would bear the task of defending and expanding freedom in the world. Kennedy claimed that this new generation did not shrink from the responsibility of defending freedom. On the contrary, the new generation (he never specifies exactly what age limits he would place on this new generation, but it would presumably include those born between 1915-1935)[31] welcomed the challenge. JFK pledged to "go anywhere, bear any burden, pay any price, meet any hardship, support any friend, and oppose any foe, to ensure the survival and success of liberty." This declaration amounted to an extraordinary blank check thrown at the feet of the world, and proved to be much farther than the American people were prepared to go. (More on this later.)

The Cairo speech parallels the Kennedy Inaugural address in the sense that it appeals to youth, and, playing to generational vanity, suggests that the youth of a particular era have a special role to play in the annals of human history. Each address revels in the fervent hope that it represents a new beginning for humanity, and a break with the tired and failed policies of the past.

The final point of comparison of the Cairo speech will be with the celebrated address delivered by President Ronald Reagan at the Brandenburg Gate on June 12, 1987. Standing at the gate in front of thousands of flag-waving spectators, with the grim specter of the Berlin Wall, symbolic of the iron fist of Soviet Communism, plainly visible in the background a few feet away, Reagan spoke clearly and eloquently about freedom and the necessity of change in the Eastern Bloc. He concluded with a challenge to Soviet strongman Mikhail Gorbachev: "Mr. Gorbachev, tear down this wall." This line, inserted personally by the President, against the wishes of State Department officials, brought a deafening cheer from the assembled crowd, who heard a clear and unmistakable anti-communist statement, delivered by the President of the United States at the center of the Cold War divide, with the world watching.

The Berlin Wall speech and Obama's Cairo effort are similar in the sense that they challenged the status quo and looked forward to the day when changes would take place and improve the world. The major difference would be the fact that Reagan chose to challenge one man to prove his dedication to peace and freedom, whereas Obama spoke in more general terms and appealed to a vague sense of understanding between nations as the precondition for lasting peace and freedom.

Chapter 5

The Point-by-Point Analysis of "A New Beginning"

Following is a point-by-point analysis of "A New Beginning." The text of the speech used in this guide can be accessed at the *Washington Post*

http://www.washingtonpost.com/wp-dyn/content/article/2009/06/04/AR2009060401117_pf.html

Except for minor deviations, it duplicates the reprint in *The Norton Reader: An Anthology of Nonfiction*, 13th edition, Linda H. Peterson, General Editor, published by W.W. Norton, copyright 2012.

President Barack Hussein Obama, Cairo University, June 4, 2009:

I am honored to be in the timeless city of Cairo, and to be hosted by two remarkable institutions. For over a thousand years, Al-Azhar has stood as a beacon of Islamic learning, and for over a century, Cairo University has been a source of Egypt's advancement. Together, you represent the harmony between tradition and progress. I am grateful for your hospitality, and the hospitality of the people of Egypt. I am also proud to carry with me the goodwill of the American people, and a greeting of peace from Muslim communities in my country: assalaamu alaykum.

Center for Islamic Pluralism: "President Obama, a Christian, has adopted the patronizing habit of addressing Muslims with Islamic greetings, citations, and blessings. These include 'assalaamu alaykum,' a reference to the Holy Qur'an, and the honorific 'peace be upon them' when discussing Moses (Musa), Jesus (Isa), and Muhammad.

"As Muslims, we consider such rhetorical trimmings by a non-Muslim speaker to be superfluous and ignorant. Muslims do not expect non-Muslims like President Obama to say 'assalaamu alaykum,' to praise Qur'an in an Islamic idiom, or to add the phrase 'peace be upon them' in speaking about God's prophets. These are artifacts of our religion. For non-Muslims to use them is gratuitous and pretentious, and appears bizarre -- as strange as it would be to hear a Muslim cleric refer to God by the Hebrew phrase 'baruch Hashem' (blessed be the creator) or say 'Jesus is Lord.'"[32]

We meet at a time of tension between the United States and Muslims around the world - tension rooted in historical forces that go beyond any current policy debate. The relationship between Islam and the West includes centuries of co-existence and cooperation, but also conflict and religious wars. More recently, tension has been fed by colonialism that denied rights and opportunities to many Muslims, and a Cold War in which Muslim-majority countries were too often treated as proxies without regard to their own aspirations. Moreover, the sweeping change brought by modernity and globalization led many Muslims to view the West as hostile to the traditions of Islam.

The truth is that the British government protected Muslims within the empire and gave implicit recognition to Islam as a religion. Pakistan, in fact, was created by the British government as a Muslim state in Northwestern India, before Britain left in 1947. India had been more of a geographical expression than a nation-state, and Britain's rule had been generally benign--except for what has become known as the Amritsar Massacre in 1919 when British troops fired on protestors who had been inflamed by Mahatma Gandhi. Pakistan literally is derived from "istan," which means "land of." Pak stands for Punjab, Afghan, and Kashmir. The British succeeded in keeping apart Muslim and Hindi fanatics, but when the British left in 1947, the religious fighting left millions dead.

The Center for Islamic Pluralism: "President Obama suggested that recent relations between the West and Islam have mainly been distorted by colonialism. But the age of colonialism in the Muslim world ended in the middle of the 20th century. Western colonialism can no longer be blamed for the problems of Muslim societies. Radical interpretations of Islam such as those of the Saudi Wahhabis, Muslim Brotherhood, Pakistani Deobandis (i.e. the Taliban), fundamentalism in Turkey, and Shia extremism present much greater problems for the West and Muslims alike, than any element of the colonial past."[33]

"...Cold War in which Muslim countries were far too often treated as proxies without regard to their aspirations..." During the Cold War the United States protected Muslim peoples from Soviet encroachment and aggression. We protected the Turks in the 40s, Iran in the 40s and 50s, Egypt in the 70s, and Afghanistan in the 80s, among other places.

The Center for Islamic Pluralism: "President Obama also stated that Muslims had, in the Cold War, been treated as proxies without regard to their own aspirations. We consider this claim offensive. The support of the U.S. for the liberation of Afghanistan from Russian occupation was not carried out in a manner indifferent to Muslim feelings.

"Notwithstanding the problems following the withdrawal of the Russians from Afghanistan, Western support for the worthy resistance of the Afghan Muslims embodied recognition of Afghan aspirations."[34]

Violent extremists have exploited these tensions in a small but potent minority of Muslims. The attacks of September 11th, 2001 and the continued efforts of these extremists to engage in violence against civilians has led some in my country to view Islam as inevitably hostile not only to America and Western countries, but also to human rights. This has bred more fear and mistrust.

So long as our relationship is defined by our differences, we will empower those who sow hatred rather than peace, and who promote conflict rather than the cooperation that can help all of our people achieve justice and prosperity. This cycle of suspicion and discord must end.

"...help all of our people achieve justice and prosperity..." Western and Islamic definitions of justice differ. The Western system of justice is based on individual rights that come from God, but are applied to all equally. Islamic society is a two-tiered society; only Muslims are equal to each other. Professor Martin Slann cites the Koran that forces non-Muslims to "pay the jizya [special tax for infidels] with willing submission" (9:29).[35] While the Western view of equal rights emanates from the Old and New Testaments of the Bible and Western philosophical traditions, no religious text is referenced when writing or implementing law. Sharia — Islamic law--in contrast, adheres strictly and literally to specific precepts in the Koran.

In Western countries like Australia and the United States, Muslim immigrants have demanded that courts, in the name of tolerance, allow the use of Sharia in domestic cases. Sharia, however, impinges on the rights of women. Andrew McCarthy notes the citing of Sharia when Muslim men abuse women who do things like venture out in public without a male escort. In the U.S. there are at least 50 cases where Islamic law has factored into rulings. In New Jersey a judge denied a protective order to a woman whose husband was serially raping and beating her. McCarthy finds Obama's close ties to Turkish Prime Minister Erdogan, who calls efforts to assimilate Muslims in Western countries "'a crime against humanity,'" troubling.[36] One must ask: Do we want Muslims to assimilate or should we tolerate such things like honor beatings and honor killings (allowed under Sharia, or Muslim law) in the United States?

I have come here to seek a new beginning between the United States and Muslims around the world; one based upon mutual interest and mutual respect; and one based upon the truth that America and Islam are not exclusive, and need not be in competition. Instead, they overlap, and share common principles - principles of justice and progress; tolerance and the dignity of all human beings.

I do so recognizing that change cannot happen overnight. No single speech can eradicate years of mistrust, nor can I answer in the time that I have all the complex questions that brought us to this point. But I am convinced that in order to move forward, we must say openly the things we hold in our hearts, and that too often are said only behind closed doors. There must be a sustained effort to listen to each other; to learn from each other; to respect one another; and to seek common ground. As the Holy Koran tells us, "Be conscious of God and speak always the truth." That is what I will try to do - to speak the truth as best I can, humbled by the task before us, and firm in my belief that the interests we share as human beings are far more powerful than the forces that drive us apart.

Raymond Ibrahim, Middle East and Islam specialist at the David Horowitz Freedom Center, points out the error in translation: "When President Barack Hussein Obama addressed the Islamic world from Cairo on June 4, 2009, he said: 'As the Holy Koran tells us, "Be conscious of God and speak always the truth" [Sura 9:119]. That is what I will try to do — to speak the truth as best I can, humbled by the task before us.' Let us for the moment put aside the fact that Sura 9, from whence Obama quotes, contains the most violent and intolerant exhortations in all the Koran. The problem here is that the original Arabic text of Sura 9:119 says absolutely nothing about 'speaking the truth.' The word 'speaking' is nowhere in the text, and 'truth,' as an abstract, is a wrong translation for SADIQIN, which refers to people. The verse most literally translates as 'fear Allah and be with the truthful.' In other words, Muslims should stand firm with fellow Muslims ('truthful' serving as a Koranic epithet for 'Muslims' the same way 'believers' often does). It is, as ever, a call for divisiveness — of Muslims (the 'truthful') versus infidels (the 'false')."[37]

The Center for Islamic Pluralism: Again, "President Obama, a Christian, has adopted the patronizing habit of addressing

Muslims with Islamic greetings, citations, and blessings. See earlier reference.[38]

Part of this conviction is rooted in my own experience. I am a Christian, but my father came from a Kenyan family that includes generations of Muslims. As a boy, I spent several years in Indonesia and heard the call of the azaan at the break of dawn and the fall of dusk. As a young man, I worked in Chicago communities where many found dignity and peace in their Muslim faith. As a student of history, I also know civilization's debt to Islam. It was Islam - at places like Al-Azhar University - that carried the light of learning through so many centuries, paving the way for Europe's Renaissance and Enlightenment. It was innovation in Muslim communities that developed the order of algebra; our magnetic compass and tools of navigation; our mastery of pens and printing; our understanding of how disease spreads and how it can be healed. Islamic culture has given us majestic arches and soaring spires; timeless poetry and cherished music; elegant calligraphy and places of peaceful contemplation. And throughout history, Islam has demonstrated through words and deeds the possibilities of religious tolerance and racial equality.

"...carried the light of learning through so many centuries, paving the way for Europe's Renaissance and Enlightenment." This is incorrect. The intellectual Renaissance began when Byzantine scholars, mostly Greek, fled the advancing Turks in the 14th century and settled in Italy. The Enlightenment was openly anti-theistic and would have been anathema to most practicing Muslims.

Obama credits the Muslims with the invention of printing, when the Chinese actually did it first.

"...Islam has demonstrated through words and deeds the possibilities of religious tolerance and racial equality." The Muslims wiped out Zoroastrianism, they battled Hinduism and Buddhism for centuries, and they levied a special tax on Christians and Jews in their domains. Under Muslim rule, pogroms were sometimes carried out against Christians and

Jews. They were also required to display special designations on clothes—Christians with a pig, Jews with a yellow Star of David—a thousand years before they were required to do so by the German Nazi government. Passages in the Koran indicate a higher estimation of light-skinned Muslims. Obama also ignores the role of Muslim traders in helping to create the African slave trade.

The classicist Victor Davis Hanson calls such claims "Obama's Islamic mythography" and contends that "Islam did not pave 'the way for Europe's Renaissance and Enlightenment.' To the extent Islam was involved at all, it was Greek scholars fleeing Ottoman pressure at Byzantium who sparked the Western Renaissance, while the Enlightenment's Romantic movements proclaimed a desire to free classical lands from supposed Ottoman backwardness." He also cites what is common knowledge among reputable historians: "Breakthroughs in navigation, pens, printing, medicine, etc. were largely Western or Chinese innovations."[39]

The writers at the Center for Islamic Pluralism also correct this obvious historical error:

> President Obama referred to the Islamic contribution to 'our (i.e. Western) mastery of pens and printing.' This is completely false. Pen and ink as we know them existed before the delivery of Qur ' an, and, for reasons open to debate, the progress of letterpress printing was delayed in the Islamic countries. These are simple facts of history. There is no point in embellishing history by denying them.[40]

Victor Davis Hanson points out this historical misrepresentation, too: "Islam has a proud tradition of tolerance. We see it in the history of Andalusia and Córdoba during the Inquisition":

> Córdoba had few Muslims when the Inquisition began in 1478, having been reconquered by the Christians well over two centuries earlier. Left unsaid was that the

great colonizers of the Middle East were not the Europeans, but the Ottoman Muslims, who were far harsher and ruled far longer.[41]

I know, too, that Islam has always been a part of America's story. The first nation to recognize my country was Morocco. In signing the Treaty of Tripoli in 1796, our second President John Adams wrote, "The United States has in itself no character of enmity against the laws, religion or tranquility of Muslims." And since our founding, American Muslims have enriched the United States. They have fought in our wars, served in government, stood for civil rights, started businesses, taught at our Universities, excelled in our sports arenas, won Nobel Prizes, built our tallest building, and lit the Olympic Torch. And when the first Muslim-American was recently elected to Congress, he took the oath to defend our Constitution using the same Holy Koran that one of our Founding Fathers - Thomas Jefferson - kept in his personal library.

Obama credits Morocco with recognizing America first, although we had earned formal recognition from France by this time. He also fails to recognize the wars between the new USA and the Barbary Pirates of North Africa, which went on for nearly thirty years.

Lawrence A. Peskin, Associate Professor of History at Morgan State University and author of *Barbary Slavery and the American Public, 1785-1816*, begins his salvo on this clear historical error with, "President Obama went to Egypt to create common ground between America and Islam. In the process he whitewashed America's early, troubled history with the Islamic world." In his recognition of American independence in 1778 and the U.S.-Tripoli treaty, Peskin charged, "the president created a mythic tale of longstanding friendship and understanding on the part of Americans and Islamic North Africans. Although it may have diplomatic uses, this tale has little historical basis." Peskin does state, "President Obama correctly stated that Morocco was the first nation to recognize American independence,"[42] but he notes that he omitted the fact that shortly thereafter Moroccans captured an American ship and its crew to force the United States to sign a pay-for-peace treaty with Morocco's ruler. The payment did not stop piracy. Obama's assertion ignored the fact that the emphasis on the non-Christian (technically) character of the nation was a strategy "to dissuade North Africans from attacking American ships."[43] When such strategy no longer worked, President Jefferson sent the Marines. The refrain from the Marine Corps Hymn "from the halls of Montezuma to the shores of Tripoli" is in reference to fighting the Muslim pirates.[44]

"And when the first Muslim-American was recently elected to Congress, he took the oath to defend our Constitution using the same Holy Koran that one of our Founding Fathers - Thomas Jefferson - kept in his personal library." President Obama here is referring to the swearing-in of Keith Ellison in 2006, when he chose the Koran instead of the Bible that had heretofore been used. At the time, the news spin was that Founding Father Thomas Jefferson, who was known for his rhetorical brilliance and deep learning, admiringly read his own copy of the Koran. Therefore, Ellison—who upset many Americans—was really doing an act that would have been considered patriotic by this Founding Father.

The reality, as was pointed out, was that Jefferson did not read the Koran for any spiritual or philosophical guidance, but to understand the thinking of the Muslim Barbary pirates in order to better fight them.

Since his first term, Ellison, a Muslim convert, has become Vice Chair of the Progressive Congressional Caucus. He had associated with the Nation of Islam in college[45] and continues with such groups as CAIR that have ties to terrorist groups.[46] According to Trevor Loudon's Key Wiki site, Ellison won approval from the Communist Party USA during his first campaign, he was greeted by the Workers World Party leader Abayomi Azikiwe during the 2008 Michigan Coalition for Human Rights annual dinner, supported lifting the Gaza blockade, met with activists who were raided by the FBI in

2010, has addressed Occupy Minneapolis, and consistently works on far-left legislation.[47] The fact that the president pointed out this highly contentious act, of defending the Constitution with the "Holy Koran" whose principles are inimical to our governing ideals, as somehow evidence of the compatibility of Islam with American ideals, however, seems to have been one lost to the few short years between 2006 and 2009. Again, Obama repeated the historical mistruth — promulgated by Keith Ellison himself — that Jefferson looked favorably upon Islam.

Human Events columnist Susan Dale Smith notes, "Not included in Obama's reference to the contents of Thomas Jefferson's library was that Jefferson also owned a much read copy of the work about Muslims entitled 'The True Nature of the Impostor Displayed,' by Humphrey Prideaux, an inveterate critic of Islam at the time."

Her column was about the 2010 White House dinner to celebrate Ramadan, where Obama asserted falsely in a speech that Jefferson had held the first Iftar dinner. Smith quotes historian Michael Oren: "Jefferson was typical of the Americans who...viewed the region [the Muslim states of North Africa] as the repository of despotism, depravity, and backwardness, a kind of inverse mirror of their own democracy, probity, and enlightenment."[48]

So I have known Islam on three continents before coming to the region where it was first revealed. That experience guides my conviction that partnership between America and Islam must be based on what Islam is, not what it isn't. And I consider it part of my responsibility as President of the United States to fight against negative stereotypes of Islam wherever they appear.

But that same principle must apply to Muslim perceptions of America. Just as Muslims do not fit a crude stereotype, America is not the crude stereotype of a self-interested empire. The United States has been one of the greatest sources of progress that the world has ever known. We were born out of revolution against an empire.

40

We were founded upon the ideal that all are created equal, and we have shed blood and struggled for centuries to give meaning to those words - within our borders, and around the world. We are shaped by every culture, drawn from every end of the Earth, and dedicated to a simple concept: E pluribus unum: "Out of many, one."

While it is true that the United States is a nation of immigrants, the fact is that the country has succeeded because those immigrants assimilated and adapted to the American form of government based on "the ideal that all are created equal," to use the President's words. While the United States has respected immigrants' rights to retain traditions through private institutions, the ideal of e pluribus unum (our national motto) has meant that old allegiances are given up. For example, American Catholics have adapted to an American system of government by placing the role of the Church in its proper sphere.

The *National Review* editors explain:

> America's Catholics once were suspected of being incompatible with an American liberty rooted in Protestantism. That incompatibility vanished when America converted Catholics here to liberty. They in turn converted the Catholic Church worldwide to liberty as well at the Second Vatican Council. Though the possibility seems remote, it is not inconceivable that America's Muslims could undergo the same evolution and eventually perform the same missionary service. For that possibility to become a fact, however, Obama would have to tell some of the hard truths of assimilation and equality to American Muslims that he diplomatically omitted when addressing the world's Muslims on Thursday.[49]

Contrary to Obama's implication, the American ideal is not one open to an Islamic, theocratic form of government and Islamic law, called Shariah. It appears that younger Muslims are resisting assimilation. While a 2007 Pew poll learned that "many Muslims . . . are highly assimilated into American society," younger Muslims are "much more likely than older Muslim Americans to say that suicide bombing in the defense of Islam can at least be justified."[50] This trend goes against the common development of previous immigrant groups, where assimilation became greater with each successive generation; in other words, while the older generation clung to their old world ways, their children became more Americanized.

The culture that we are shaped by is decidedly the Western one, with a justice system based on individual rights. The cultures that come here are forced to adhere to the Western (more specifically, British-influenced, legal system). Our courts up until now have not recognized the legal standards of the countries of the immigrants' origins. But many Muslim advocacy groups are working to implement parallel legal systems for Muslims. Some judges have already applied Shariah in domestic cases.

Much has been made of the fact that an African-American with the name Barack Hussein Obama could be elected President. But my personal story is not so unique. The dream of opportunity for all people has not come true for everyone in America, but its promise exists for all who come to our shores - that includes nearly seven million American Muslims in our country today who enjoy incomes and education that are higher than average.

The Center for Islamic Pluralism: "We do not accept as credible the claim, excessive in our view, that American Muslims total seven million people. This is a highly controversial issue and the numbers of our community in the United States need not be exaggerated."[51] The 2007 Pew poll, cited by Professor Slann previously, put the number at 2.35 million. Professor Furnish noted the later 2011 poll, showing 2.75 million Muslims in America.

Moreover, freedom in America is indivisible from the freedom to practice one's religion. That is why there is a mosque in every state of our union, and over 1,200 mosques within our borders. That is why the U.S. government has gone to court to protect the right of women and girls to wear the hijab, and to punish those who would deny it.

Obama is right to praise the freedom to practice religion and is to be commended for pointing out the fact that Muslims enjoy this freedom in the United States. But this is not a freedom granted to Christians and Jews in many Muslim countries. While certainly the wearing of a hijab is a right that most Americans agree is protected by the First Amendment, one must ask about other symbols of female oppression under Islam, like the anonymity of the burqa and female genital cutting forced on under-age girls. Islamic dress that obscures identity conflicts with the ideals of freedom and equality that Obama referenced. An open society requires free communication and identity. Because it obscures the face completely, the burqa obscures identity and interferes with communication by hiding facial expressions. The freedom to come and go unrestrictedly and to engage in commerce comes with the duty to identify oneself to fellow citizens. For example, when engaging in banking transactions one must produce picture ID. Most banks, for security purposes, do not allow the wearing of facial coverings, like ski masks. While the U.S. does allow wide latitude on dress, one can see the necessity for certain restrictions.

Such minimal restrictions contrast with the religious police in Saudi Arabia and Iran, who monitor such forbidden behavior as hand-holding between husband and wife in public and harass women not wearing veil or hijab.[52]

National Review editors:

> His defense of the right of Muslim women to wear the hijab against (we suppose) Western authorities, such as the French government, which restrict it was a cheap shot. Some governments of Muslim countries also restrict traditional dress, such as successive Kemalist

governments in Turkey, and others such as Saudi Arabia insist on sartorial anonymity for women.[53]

So let there be no doubt: Islam is a part of America. And I believe that America holds within her the truth that regardless of race, religion, or station in life, all of us share common aspirations - to live in peace and security; to get an education and to work with dignity; to love our families, our communities, and our God. These things we share. This is the hope of all humanity.

The assumption that all of humanity shares these Western goals is part of the political aspect of this speech that the editors of *National Review* noted. While the impulse to find a common ground is laudable, the fact remains that the majority of cultures across the globe do not share such Western values as tolerance, respect for human rights, equality, free association, and private property. President Obama might be accused in the same manner that George W. Bush was of projecting his own Western democratic values onto other cultures that sometimes don't welcome them.

Of course, recognizing our common humanity is only the beginning of our task. Words alone cannot meet the needs of our people. These needs will be met only if we act boldly in the years ahead; and if we understand that the challenges we face are shared, and our failure to meet them will hurt us all.

These are inspirational words, as to be expected and welcomed from a president. But the real outcomes of this speech and the presidential actions will be investigated later.

For we have learned from recent experience that when a financial system weakens in one country, prosperity is hurt everywhere. When a new flu infects one human being, all are at risk. When one nation pursues a nuclear weapon, the risk of nuclear attack rises for all nations. When violent extremists operate in one stretch of mountains, people are endangered across an ocean. And when innocents in Bosnia and Darfur are slaughtered, that is a stain on our collective conscience. That is what it means to share this world in the 21st century. That is the responsibility we have to one another as human beings.

Is the analogy between a disease and financial well-being true or false? Certainly, since the twentieth century recessions and depressions have spread worldwide. Obama is referring to the Taliban and Al Qaeda whose leaders strategized in the mountains of Afghanistan for the 9/11 attacks. One might counter Obama's assertion by stating that a strong national defense can ensure that terrorists living in remote mountains cannot invade. Ways to ensure a country's security include protecting national borders, providing strong security checks, and maintaining a strong military force. Obama is here alluding to his campaign claim of being a "citizen of the world." Some might take issue with the idea of a "collective conscience" and its very possibility. But one must ask: Is it logical to place guilt on the U.S. for tribal genocide in Darfur? The ethnic cleansing in the Darfur region of Sudan is a continuation of Muslim practices of ethnic cleansing, especially against the Jews, since the time of Mohammad.

The postulate, "When one nation pursues a nuclear weapon, the risk of nuclear attack rises for all nations," is debatable. Is the analogy to the highly contagious disease of the flu true or false? Is Obama making a logical fallacy in this analogy? Some would argue that having a strong nuclear arsenal acts as a deterrent to the spread of nuclear threats. It actually prevents the spread of nuclear threats and acts in a manner opposite to disease contagion. For example, if the Germans had gotten the bomb before we got it they would likely have used it on us, just as they launched the V-2 rockets against London in 1944. Similarly, no nation has considered a pre-emptive strike against another nuclear power.

This is a difficult responsibility to embrace. For human history has often been a record of nations and tribes subjugating one another to serve their own interests. Yet in this new age, such attitudes are self-defeating. Given our interdependence, any world order that elevates one nation or group of people over another will inevitably fail. So whatever we think of the past, we must not be prisoners of it. Our problems must be dealt with through partnership; progress must be shared.

The reference to an international "interdependence" raises the question about American sovereignty and exceptionalism. The idea of "partnership" is vague. It could mean partnership in terms of free trade, as President Washington would claim. Or it might mean subjugating American law to international law, for which many Obama appointees have argued. Most would maintain that the United States, with its institutions that implement ideals of Western law and ethics, is an exception to other systems that operate on principles of power and prejudice. In countries lacking the necessary qualities, the people often "democratically" elect despots. Should the U.S. compromise her own ideals for such "interdependence"?

While certainly one should not be a "prisoner" of the past, looking to the past, to history, has served our country well. The Founding Fathers resisted the revolutionary currents that were inflaming the French Revolution, and wisely and judiciously searched in history for models of successful government. Such an approach has resulted in a Constitution that is the longest lasting in the world, with peaceful transitions of power after regular and free elections.

That does not mean we should ignore sources of tension. Indeed, it suggests the opposite: we must face these tensions squarely. And so in that spirit, let me speak as clearly and plainly as I can about some specific issues that I believe we must finally confront together.

The first issue that we have to confront is violent extremism in all of its forms.

In Ankara, I made clear that America is not - and never will be - at war with Islam. We will, however, relentlessly confront violent extremists who pose a grave threat to our security. Because we reject the same thing that people of all faiths reject: the killing of innocent men, women, and children. And it is my first duty as President to protect the American people.

46

"America is not at war with Islam": Again, refer to the *Washington Times* editorial that cites a few of the many similar statements made by George W. Bush.[54]

Obama does say, correctly, "It is my first duty to protect the American people." In regards to the President's duties under the Constitution, and the manner in which he is to protect the people, we can start with the traditional oath of office: "I do solemnly swear that I will faithfully execute the Office of President of the United states, and will to the best of my ability, preserve, protect, and defend the Constitution of the United States."

Article II, section 2, makes the President the Commander-In-Chief of the armed forces, and empowers him with the authority to repel an attack on the territory of the United States without first going to Congress. A declaration of war requires Congressional approval, but Presidents have had wide latitude in calling the military into service, when in the performance of their duties in "protecting the country from all foes, foreign or domestic."

The situation in Afghanistan demonstrates America's goals, and our need to work together. Over seven years ago, the United States pursued al Qaeda and the Taliban with broad international support. We did not go by choice, we went because of necessity. I am aware that some question or justify the events of 9/11. But let us be clear: al Qaeda killed nearly 3,000 people on that day. The victims were innocent men, women and children from America and many other nations who had done nothing to harm anybody. And yet Al Qaeda chose to ruthlessly murder these people, claimed credit for the attack, and even now states their determination to kill on a massive scale. They have affiliates in many countries and are trying to expand their reach. These are not opinions to be debated; these are facts to be dealt with.

This statement is true: those killed on 9/11 represented a cross-section of American society, including Muslims. Obama is right to state that such an attack warrants nothing other than unequivocal condemnation.

Make no mistake: we do not want to keep our troops in Afghanistan. We seek no military bases there. It is agonizing for America to lose our young men and women. It is costly and politically difficult to continue this conflict. We would gladly bring every single one of our troops home if we could be confident that there were not violent extremists in Afghanistan and Pakistan determined to kill as many Americans as they possibly can. But that is not yet the case.

That's why we're partnering with a coalition of forty-six countries. And despite the costs involved, America's commitment will not weaken. Indeed, none of us should tolerate these extremists. They have killed in many countries. They have killed people of different faiths - more than any other, they have killed Muslims. Their actions are irreconcilable with the rights of human beings, the progress of nations, and with Islam. The Holy Koran teaches that whoever kills an innocent, it is as if he has killed all mankind; and whoever saves a person, it is as if he has saved all mankind. The enduring faith of over a billion people is so much bigger than the narrow hatred of a few. Islam is not part of the problem in combating violent extremism - it is an important part of promoting peace.

Within Islam are many factions that have been fighting each other for centuries. The largest battles occur between Sunnis and Shiites. Andrew McCarthy, the chief prosecutor of the 1993 World Trade Center bombing, has repeatedly given credit to the peaceful Muslim-Americans who provided valuable information to the police and FBI in tracking down terrorists.[55] However, Obama may be playing loose with theological interpretations here, selectively alluding to the Koran in order to make an overly simplistic claim for his political purposes. Again, what must be balanced in such a speech is adherence to precise scholarly interpretations and political goals.

We also know that military power alone is not going to solve the problems in Afghanistan and Pakistan. That is why we plan to *invest $1.5 billion each year over the next five years to partner with Pakistanis to build schools and hospitals, roads and businesses, and hundreds of millions to help those who have been displaced. And that is why we are providing more than $2.8 billion to help Afghans develop their economy and deliver services that people depend upon.*

As far as warfare: We fought to protect Muslims in Kuwait in 1990-91, in Bosnia from 1992-1999, in Somalia in 1992-94, and from 2002-2012 in the new Middle Eastern War.

Let me also address the issue of Iraq. Unlike Afghanistan, Iraq was a war of choice that provoked strong differences in my country and around the world. Although I believe that the Iraqi people are ultimately better off without the tyranny of Saddam Hussein, I also believe that events in Iraq have reminded America of the need to use diplomacy and build international consensus to resolve our problems whenever possible. Indeed, we can recall the words of Thomas Jefferson, who said: "I hope that our wisdom will grow with our power, and teach us that the less we use our power the greater it will be."

He criticizes President George W. Bush harshly by stating, "Iraq was a war of choice" and implies that Bush led the nation to war illegitimately and needlessly. The reference to the need for international consensus carries the danger of threatening American sovereignty and independence. No American president has ever ceded authority to an international body.

By the use of Thomas Jefferson's quotation, Obama implies that Jefferson would have agreed with his internationalist approach. Nicholas J. Cull, Professor of Public Diplomacy at the University of Southern California, traces the Jefferson quotation to a letter Jefferson wrote to Thomas Leiper as he learned that Napoleon Bonaparte had escaped from his exile on the island of Elba, landed in France and marched on Paris to become Emperor once more. Leiper, a Scott, had rather enjoyed the impending discomfort to the tyrannical English government. Replying in June 1815, Jefferson cautioned him that Bonaparte was no friend of America either. Rather than endorsing either England or France, Jefferson expressed his hope:

> ...that all nations may recover and retain their independence; that those which are overgrown may not advance beyond safe measures of power, that a salutary balance may be maintained among nations, and that our peace, commerce and friendship, may be sought and cultivated by all.

Leiper explains, "Jefferson looked to a future of American ascendancy: 'Not in our day, but at no distant one, we may shake the rod over the heads of all, which may make the stoutest of them tremble.' Then comes the now familiar Cairo quote: 'But I hope our wisdom will grow with our power, and teach us, that the less we use our power, the greater it will be.'"[56]

Again, while Jefferson expressed the hope that a peaceful coexistence would prevail, when it came time to protect American interests Jefferson took the necessary independent actions. He approached Britain for help on fighting the Barbary pirates, but when she refused he took decisive independent military action.

Today, America has a dual responsibility: to help Iraq forge a better future - and to leave Iraq to Iraqis. I have made it clear to the Iraqi people that we pursue no bases, and no claim on their territory or resources. Iraq's sovereignty is its own. That is why I ordered the removal of our combat brigades by next August. That is why we will honor our agreement with Iraq's democratically-elected government to remove combat troops from Iraqi cities by July, and to remove all our troops from Iraq by 2012. We will help Iraq train its Security Forces and develop its economy. But we will support a secure and united Iraq as a partner, and never as a patron.

President George W. Bush, in his address of March 19, 2003, on the start of the Iraq war, said, "We come to Iraq with respect for its citizens, for their great civilization and for the religious faiths they practice. We have no ambition in Iraq except to remove a threat and restore control of that country to its own people."[57]

On September 7 of that year, he said,

> America has done this kind of work before. Following World War II, we lifted up the defeated nations of Japan and Germany, and stood with them as they built representative governments. We committed years and resources to this cause. And that effort has been repaid many times over in three generations of friendship and peace. America today accepts the challenge of helping Iraq in the same spirit -- for their sake, and our own.[58]

He repeated the same sentiments in 2007 during the surge and at points in between.

Many critics, however, have pointed to Obama's announcement of a pull-out date as a dangerous tip-off to insurgents and terrorists.

Immediately after the pullout in July 2009, attacks by insurgents escalated, as predicted by military and political leaders. Former Ambassador John Bolton wrote that our withdrawal empowered Iran, escalating that regime's terrorist attacks throughout the region:

> Iran has already substantially increased its meddling inside Iraq, both influencing the regime of Nouri al-Maliki and enhancing the capabilities of terrorist thugs like Muqtada al-Sadr. It is challenging its Arab neighbours across the Gulf, threatening to close the Straits of Hormuz and target the US bases and facilities there (as well as Nato forces in Turkey).

Tehran was working to keep Syrian dictator Assad in power, and Hezbollah effectively in control in Lebanon, while developing nuclear weapons.[59]

And finally, just as America can never tolerate violence by extremists, we must never alter our principles. 9/11 was an enormous trauma to our country. The fear and anger that it provoked was understandable, but in some cases, it led us to act contrary to our ideals. We are taking concrete actions to change course. I have unequivocally prohibited the use of torture by the United States, and I have ordered the prison at Guantanamo Bay closed by early next year.

Closing the POW camp at Guantanamo was a campaign promise. Nearly three years after the Cairo speech, Khalid Sheikh Mohammed, the mastermind of the 9/11 attacks, was brought to trial—at Guantanamo, where he and others had been held. The *Wall Street Journal* editors faulted the Obama administration for interfering with the course set by George W. Bush in 2008, a time when KSM pleaded guilty and expressed his desire to die as a martyr. The Obama administration tried to move the terrorists to civilian court in New York, a plan that "foundered on bipartisan political opposition."[60] The proposals to house these prisoners of war in institutions on U.S. soil were met with widespread alarm.

So America will defend itself respectful of the sovereignty of nations and the rule of law. And we will do so in partnership with Muslim communities which are also threatened. The sooner the extremists are isolated and unwelcome in Muslim communities, the sooner we will all be safer.

The second major source of tension that we need to discuss is the situation between Israelis, Palestinians and the Arab world.

America's strong bonds with Israel are well known. This bond is based upon cultural and historical ties, and the recognition that the aspiration for a Jewish homeland is rooted in a tragic history that cannot be denied.

The United States assisted the Jews in reestablishing their homeland in the Middle East in 1948, after the genocide by the Nazis in World War II—the "tragic history." Israel has since been a dependable ally of the United States. The cultural and historical ties go back to Biblical times. Jesus Christ was a Jew, and the New Testament is seen by Christians as fulfillment of the Old Testament, called the Torah by the Jews. It is no coincidence that our culture is referred to as the Judeo-Christian culture, one based on the monotheistic belief of a God who revealed Himself first to the Jews. Our customs, laws, and values have much in common. Obama is correct in pointing out these important facts.

Around the world, the Jewish people were persecuted for centuries, and anti-Semitism in Europe culminated in an unprecedented Holocaust. Tomorrow, I will visit Buchenwald, which was part of a network of camps where Jews were enslaved, tortured, shot and gassed to death by the Third Reich. Six million Jews were killed - more than the entire Jewish population of Israel today. Denying that fact is baseless, ignorant, and hateful. Threatening Israel with destruction - or repeating vile stereotypes about Jews - is deeply wrong, and only serves to evoke in the minds of Israelis this most painful of memories while preventing the peace that the people of this region deserve.

While Obama is correct to point out the anti-Semitism in Europe, his omissions of alliances between the German Nazis and Muslims skews this history and make it appear that anti-Semitism was confined to Europe. Anti-Semitism emerged during the 1880s, but more so in Russia and France than in Germany-Austria-Hungary. After German defeat in World War I, Jews, especially financiers, became the scapegoats. Before then, in Germany Jews were fairly well treated, with many making up Vienna's upper middle class. It was a Jewish-German general who awarded Adolf Hitler his second Iron Cross during World War I. As with other groups, prejudice arose within ranks, with German Jews often looking down on their Russian and Polish counterparts. During the Nazi regime, many European Christians hid Jews at great risk to their own lives.

History shows widespread Muslim persecution of Jews and ties to the Nazi regime. Under Muslim rule, Christian and Jewish communities were required to pay a special jizya tax and to affix their doors with images of the devil.[61] Nazi military and police commander Heinrich Himmler and Muslim leader of Palestine Haj Amin al-Husseini met several times, and Al-Husseini urged the regime to pursue the elimination of European Jews.[62] Hitler's *Mein Kampf*, which is banned in several European countries, is a bestseller in its Arabic translation in several Middle Eastern countries.

On the other hand, it is also undeniable that the Palestinian people - Muslims and Christians - have suffered in pursuit of a homeland. For more than sixty years they have endured the pain of dislocation. Many wait in refugee camps in the West Bank, Gaza, and neighboring lands for a life of peace and security that they have never been able to lead. They endure the daily humiliations - large and small - that come with occupation. So let there be no doubt: the situation for the Palestinian people is intolerable. America will not turn our backs on the legitimate Palestinian aspiration for dignity, opportunity, and a state of their own.

Many historians and political scientists would disagree with Obama's categorization of an "occupation." He ignores the recent concessions by Israel to give over land in the West Bank. He ignores the civil liberties the Palestinian refugees enjoy and the dangers of terrorism coming from Gaza.

For decades, there has been a stalemate: two peoples with legitimate aspirations, each with a painful history that makes compromise elusive. It is easy to point fingers - for Palestinians to point to the displacement brought by Israel's founding, and for Israelis to point to the constant hostility and attacks throughout its history from within its borders as well as beyond. But if we see this conflict only from one side or the other, then we will be blind to the truth: the only resolution is for the aspirations of both sides to be met through two states, where Israelis and Palestinians each live in peace and security.

That is in Israel's interest, Palestine's interest, America's interest, and the world's interest. That is why I intend to personally pursue this outcome with all the patience that the task requires. The obligations that the parties have agreed to under the Road Map are clear. For peace to come, it is time for them - and all of us - to live up to our responsibilities.

Palestinians must abandon violence. Resistance through violence and killing is wrong and does not succeed. For centuries, black people in America suffered the lash of the whip as slaves and the humiliation of segregation. But it was not violence that won full and equal rights. It was a peaceful and determined insistence upon the ideals at the center of America's founding. This same story can be told by people from South Africa to South Asia; from Eastern Europe to Indonesia. It's a story with a simple truth: that violence is a dead end. It is a sign of neither courage nor power to shoot rockets at sleeping children, or to blow up old women on a bus. That is not how moral authority is claimed; that is how it is surrendered.

Most would praise Obama for calling on the Palestinians to end violence. However, the analogy to the Civil Rights movement is historically inaccurate. While it is true that "violence" was not what "won full and equal rights" in the U.S., it is true because those who used the legal system and protested peacefully were able to appeal to the founding principles and were protected by American law. Frederick Douglass and Martin Luther King, Jr., for example, both cited the Declaration of Independence in their famous calls for racial equality, "What to the Slave is the Fourth of July?" and "Letter from Birmingham Jail," respectively. The same was not the case in other parts of the world that did not enjoy our Constitutional form of government. Certainly, the citizens of the countries of the Soviet Bloc could not march and petition for equal rights, because they knew that the result would be torture and death. Protest movements, like the one in Hungary in 1956, were squelched with Soviet tanks, resulting in the deaths of thousands. Contrary to Obama's claim, the people of Eastern Europe did not share the "same story." In fact, it wasn't until the Soviet Union collapsed that those countries were able to enjoy "full and equal rights."

Now is the time for Palestinians to focus on what they can build. The Palestinian Authority must develop its capacity to govern, with institutions that serve the needs of its people. Hamas does have support among some Palestinians, but they also have responsibilities. To play a role in fulfilling Palestinian aspirations, and to unify the Palestinian people, Hamas must put an end to violence, recognize past agreements, and recognize Israel's right to exist.

At the same time, Israelis must acknowledge that just as Israel's right to exist cannot be denied, neither can Palestine's. The United States does not accept the legitimacy of continued Israeli settlements. This construction violates previous agreements and undermines efforts to achieve peace. It is time for these settlements to stop.

"...just as Israel's right to exist cannot be denied, neither can Palestine's." Jordan was created as the Palestinian Arab Muslim state already in 1948. When the Zionist movement began in the 1880s, places like South Africa, Madagascar, and Siberia, were considered as possibilities of sites for a Jewish state. The Jews could not go back to their original Middle Eastern homeland because it was occupied by Turkey. The British signed the Balfour Declaration in 1916 that in principle marked a Jewish homeland (not state) contingent upon victory in the war. The League of Nations mandated that Palestine be a British territory, but not in perpetuity. Although the British tried to keep them out, the Jews settled there. The idea of a Jewish state became more urgent after World War II, and Jewish settlers evicted the British. The United Nations then allocated land west of the Jordan River as Israel and the east as Jordan, a Palestinian Arabic Muslim state.

In the late 1980s, the Soviets allowed the emigration of Jews to Israel, where they started building (illegally) on the West Bank.

Obama makes no note of the fact that Israel allows the free practice of Islam within her boundaries, but that the Palestinians deny rights of worship to Jews and Christians in Palestine.

The Middle East has been a hostile place for Christians. The percentage of the population that is Christian has dropped from 15 percent in 1950 to 3 percent in 2010.

Israel must also live up to its obligations to ensure that Palestinians can live, and work, and develop their society. And just as it devastates Palestinian families, the continuing humanitarian crisis in Gaza does not serve Israel's security; neither does the continuing lack of opportunity in the West Bank. Progress in the daily lives of the Palestinian people must be part of a road to peace, and Israel must take concrete steps to enable such progress.

Finally, the Arab States must recognize that the Arab Peace Initiative was an important beginning, but not the end of their responsibilities. The Arab-Israeli conflict should no longer be used to distract the people of Arab nations from other problems. Instead, it must be a cause for action to help the Palestinian people develop the institutions that will sustain their state; to recognize Israel's legitimacy; and to choose progress over a self-defeating focus on the past.

Obama here juxtaposes the two sides and calls out the duties for each in skillful balance.

America will align our policies with those who pursue peace, and say in public what we say in private to Israelis and Palestinians and Arabs. We cannot impose peace. But privately, many Muslims recognize that Israel will not go away. Likewise, many Israelis recognize the need for a Palestinian state. It is time for us to act on what everyone knows to be true. Too many tears have flowed. Too much blood has been shed. All of us have a responsibility to work for the day when the mothers of Israelis and Palestinians can see their children grow up without fear; when the Holy Land of three great faiths is the place of peace that God intended it to be; when Jerusalem is a secure and lasting home for Jews and Christians and Muslims, and a place for all of the children of Abraham to mingle peacefully together as in the story of Isra, when Moses, Jesus, and Mohammed (peace be upon them) joined in prayer.

Obama makes an effective emotional appeal (pathos) here with the detailed references to the images of blood being shed, and mothers with their children. Obama, however, does not cite a source for his claim that God intended the Holy Land to be place of peace for the "three great faiths." Each of the three faiths stakes a claim on the land, but neither faith holds the belief that it is there for all three faiths.

Center for Islamic Pluralism: The writers see the use of the Muslim saying, "peace be upon them," as "patronizing."[63]

The third source of tension is our shared interest in the rights and responsibilities of nations on nuclear weapons.

This issue has been a source of tension between the United States and the Islamic Republic of Iran. For many years, Iran has defined itself in part by its opposition to my country, and there is indeed a tumultuous history between us. In the middle of the Cold War, the United States played a role in the overthrow of a democratically-elected Iranian government. Since the Islamic Revolution, Iran has played a role in acts of hostage-taking and violence against U.S. troops and civilians. This history is well known. Rather than remain trapped in the past, I have made it clear to Iran's leaders and people that my country is prepared to move forward. The question, now, is not what Iran is against, but rather what future it wants to build.

The characterization of the role of the United States during the Cold War is not entirely correct. It is true that in 1953 the CIA overthrew Prime Minister Mussadiq whose powers, along with those of the legislature, grew and threatened the regime of Mohammed Reza Shah. But Mussadiq's era was marked by turmoil and unrest. The fact that there was the menace of the Soviet Union bordering on the north played into the coup. Britain, who had removed his father, Reza Shah, from power in 1941, persuaded the U.S. to initiate the coup, which was followed by Western investments in an oil consortium and massive American military and economic aid as part of the Eisenhower Doctrine's policy of building strong and stable anti-communist regimes around the world. While the Shah did rely on the military to keep order and to keep the Ayatollah Khomeini in check, he also instituted Western freedoms and advancements.[64] When the Ayatollah came into power in 1979, Western freedoms, especially for women, were abolished under his Muslim theocratic rule. It should be noted that Obama didn't oppose the stolen election in Iran in 2009, even while protestors in the U.S. asked him to.

It will be hard to overcome decades of mistrust, but we will proceed with courage, rectitude and resolve. There will be many issues to discuss between our two countries, and we are willing to move forward without preconditions on the basis of mutual respect. But it is clear to all concerned that when it comes to nuclear weapons, we have reached a decisive point. This is not simply about America's interests. It is about preventing a nuclear arms race in the Middle East that could lead this region and the world down a hugely dangerous path.

I understand those who protest that some countries have weapons that others do not. No single nation should pick and choose which nations hold nuclear weapons. That is why I strongly reaffirmed America's commitment to seek a world in which no nations hold nuclear weapons. And any nation - including Iran - should have the right to access peaceful nuclear power if it complies with its responsibilities under the nuclear Non-Proliferation Treaty. That commitment is at the core of the Treaty, and it must be kept for all who fully abide by it. And I am hopeful that all countries in the region can share in this goal.

While it might be nice to wish for "a world in which no nations hold nuclear weapons," the possibility of it, often repeated by peace protestors who would like the U.S. to lead the way, is distant. Here, Obama, however, treats Iran, a nation whose leaders have repeatedly vowed to destroy Israel, as being on the same moral plane as others, say France. Iran has repeatedly lied about its adherence to the nuclear Non-Proliferation Treaty. To affirm Iran's equal standing in the face of such reality struck many commentators as outrageous.

The fourth issue that I will address is democracy.

I know there has been controversy about the promotion of democracy in recent years, and much of this controversy is connected to the war in Iraq. So let me be clear: no system of government can or should be imposed upon one nation by any other.

Victor Davis Hanson asks about the sentence, "No system of government can or should be imposed upon one nation by any other." He wonders, "Would that include postwar Japan, Italy, and Germany? Should we not have attempted to impose a system of government in Iraq or Afghanistan?"[65]

That does not lessen my commitment, however, to governments that reflect the will of the people. Each nation gives life to this principle in its own way, grounded in the traditions of its own people. America does not presume to know what is best for everyone, just as we would not presume to pick the outcome of a peaceful election. But I do have an unyielding belief that all people yearn for certain things: the ability to speak your mind and have a say in how you are governed; confidence in the rule of law and the equal administration of justice; government that is transparent and doesn't steal from the people; the freedom to live as you choose. Those are not just American ideas, they are human rights, and that is why we will support them everywhere.

The idea of human rights as we know them today were adapted from Western and American ideals. Shariah differs greatly. Not "all people" yearn for free speech, self-rule, equal justice, and freedom in lifestyle choices, as Obama believes. In fact, these are the aspects of American society that Islamic theocrats despise.

There is no straight line to realize this promise. But this much is clear: governments that protect these rights are ultimately more stable, successful and secure. Suppressing ideas never succeeds in making them go away. America respects the right of all peaceful and law-abiding voices to be heard around the world, even if we disagree with them. And we will welcome all elected, peaceful governments - provided they govern with respect for all their people.

This last point is important because there are some who advocate for democracy only when they are out of power; once in power, they are ruthless in suppressing the rights of others. No matter where it takes hold, government of the people and by the people sets a single standard for all who hold power: you must maintain your power through consent, not coercion; you must respect the rights of minorities, and participate with a spirit of tolerance and compromise; you must place the interests of your people and the legitimate workings of the political process above your party. Without these ingredients, elections alone do not make true democracy. Without these ingredients, elections can result in despotism.

The fifth issue that we must address together is religious freedom.

Islam has a proud tradition of tolerance. We see it in the history of Andalusia and Cordoba during the Inquisition. I saw it firsthand as a child in Indonesia, where devout Christians worshiped freely in an overwhelmingly Muslim country. That is the spirit we need today. People in every country should be free to choose and live their faith based upon the persuasion of the mind, heart, and soul. This tolerance is essential for religion to thrive, but it is being challenged in many different ways.

"Islam has a proud history of tolerance." The founder of Islam, Muhammad, after being unsuccessful with peaceful means of conversion, used violence. Islam has been spread by the sword, beginning with Abu-Bakr's conquest of the un-reconciled tribes of southern and eastern Arabia for Islam. In 638, Jerusalem was conquered by Islam. In 732, a Muslim army was deep into France, when it was turned back because of communication problems and the encroaching winter. Their commander was killed by the Franks. "The Islamic onslaught in the West remains an astonishing achievement," writes J.M. Roberts.[66]

The footnotes in the Norton anthology casually note the Spanish Inquisition as a Tribunal established to enforce

Catholic orthodoxy. The Spanish Inquisition was, in fact, a royal organ, not a church institution.

Victor Davis Hanson: "'Islam has a proud tradition of tolerance. We see it in the history of Andalusia and Córdoba during the Inquisition.' Córdoba had few Muslims when the Inquisition began in 1478, having been reconquered by the Christians well over two centuries earlier. Left unsaid was that the great colonizers of the Middle East were not the Europeans, but the Ottoman Muslims, who were far harsher and ruled far longer."[67]

Center for Islamic Pluralism: "President Obama referred, under the rhetoric of Islamic tolerance, to 'the history of Andalusia and Cordoba during the Inquisition.' First, Cordoba is located in Andalusia, and is not separate from it. Second, there was no 'tolerance' by Muslims during the Spanish National Inquisition, in which Muslims and Jews were subjected to broken promises and brutal persecution as victims of intolerance. This appears as yet another jarring example of a gaffe by the president, involving a widely-known chapter in history. The situation of the three religions in Spain from 711 CE to the mid-17th century, when the last open Muslim believers were driven out of Spain, is a serious and demanding topic that does not lend itself to improvisation."[68]

Dr. Timothy Furnish adds, "Insofar as tolerance and diversity did exist [in Andalusia], it was not because of inherent Islamic proclivities but because under the 'petty [Muslim] state' in the Iberian peninsula the majority of the population remained Christian — and in order to keep them in line, forced conversions were the exception. Nonetheless, Islamic law operated and many churches were converted into mosques. And all pretense of 'toleration' collapsed under al-Muwahhid (Almohad) rule, 1130-1269 AD, when the followers of Ibn Tumart, the 'Mahdi' from North Africa, enforced a harsh brand of Islam in which Christians in particular were actively persecuted and killed in Iberia and North Africa. (See my book Holiest Wars, pp. 31-38.)"[69]

Among some Muslims, there is a disturbing tendency to measure one's own faith by the rejection of another's. The richness of religious diversity must be upheld - whether it is for Maronites in Lebanon or the Copts in Egypt. And fault lines must be closed among Muslims as well, as the divisions between Sunni and Shia have led to tragic violence, particularly in Iraq.

Freedom of religion is central to the ability of peoples to live together. We must always examine the ways in which we protect it. For instance, in the United States, rules on charitable giving have made it harder for Muslims to fulfill their religious obligation. That is why I am committed to working with American Muslims to ensure that they can fulfill zakat. Likewise, it is important for Western countries to avoid impeding Muslim citizens from practicing religion as they see fit - for instance, by dictating what clothes a Muslim woman should wear. We cannot disguise hostility towards any religion behind the pretence of liberalism.

President Obama is right to urge all to allow freedom of religion, but he misrepresents Muslim charity, or zakat. The Norton anthology, in a footnote, describes zakat as "Obligation to give alms, one of the Five Pillars of Islam." According to the site for Muslims, "Mission Islam," zakat refers to "the name of what a believer returns out of his or her wealth to the neediest of *Muslims* for the sake of the Almighty Allah" [emphasis added].[70] The footnote in the textbook neglects to mention that such charity is intended for Muslims only. There are no such limitations on charity in the Old and New Testaments.

Jerry Gordon, writing at the *New English Review*, notes that "Zakat recipients would include the poor and needy, administrators of Zakat, debtors, converts to Islam, bondsmen, wayfarers and those fulfilling the 'way of Allah,' Jihad." He quotes from *Mission Islam*: "By this is meant to finance a Jihad effort in the path of Allah, not for Jihad for other reasons. The fighter (Mujahid) will be given as salary what will be enough for him. If he needs to buy arms or some other supplies related to the war effort, Zakat money should be used provided the effort is to raise the banner of Islam."

"It is the application of Zakat proceeds to Jihad, especially in the US, that is most problematic," Gordon writes, and speculates that Obama's claims about the unfairness regarding rules on charitable giving was in response to a preview of an ACLU report that claimed that the U.S. government's clamp-down on Islamic terrorist groups disguising themselves as charitable organizations was unfair.[71]

Indeed, faith should bring us together. That is why we are forging service projects in America that bring together Christians, Muslims, and Jews. That is why we welcome efforts like Saudi Arabian King Abdullah's Interfaith dialogue and Turkey's leadership in the Alliance of Civilizations. Around the world, we can turn dialogue into Interfaith service, so bridges between peoples lead to action - whether it is combating malaria in Africa, or providing relief after a natural disaster.

The sixth issue that I want to address is women's rights.

I know there is debate about this issue. I reject the view of some in the West that a woman who chooses to cover her hair is somehow less equal, but I do believe that a woman who is denied an education is denied equality. And it is no coincidence that countries where women are well-educated are far more likely to be prosperous.

Now let me be clear: issues of women's equality are by no means simply an issue for Islam. In Turkey, Pakistan, Bangladesh and Indonesia, we have seen Muslim-majority countries elect a woman to lead. Meanwhile, the struggle for women's equality continues in many aspects of American life, and in countries around the world.

Our daughters can contribute just as much to society as our sons, and our common prosperity will be advanced by allowing all humanity - men and women - to reach their full potential. I do not believe that women must make the same choices as men in order to be equal, and I respect those women who choose to live their lives in traditional roles. But it should be their choice. That is why the United States will partner with any Muslim-majority country to support expanded literacy for girls, and to help young women pursue employment through micro-financing that helps people live their dreams.

"...avoid impeding Muslim citizens from practicing their religion as they see fit, by dictating what clothes a Muslim woman should wear..." President Obama implies that women in Muslim and Western countries face the same challenges to equality. The Muslim world has traditionally rejected Western notions of women's rights. In the strict Islamic understanding a woman is the legal property of her husband. In the more reactionary Muslim states, Saudi Arabia, for instance, women cannot vote, they cannot hold public office, they have only recently been granted the right to drive automobiles, and their rights to hold paid employment are strictly limited.

In Saudi Arabia, Islamic principles clashed with modernism twice in recent years. The Saudi regime bowed to international pressure and reluctantly allowed women to operate motor vehicles. This followed highly publicized incidents wherein foreign women, many in the diplomatic service, were cited by Saudi police for breaking the driving laws. A public outcry followed, and the Saudi government decided to grant drivers licenses to women, but with many restrictions.

The issue of paid employment also saw twin Islamic principles crashing headlong into each other. Saudi women could not hold paid employment. It was a serious violation of the law. This principle, however, brushed up against the equally dear Islamic notion of feminine modesty. Saudi women visiting lingerie shops were shocked and embarrassed at the fact that they would divulge intimate details about themselves and their bodies to male sales clerks, when buying their underwear. This presented the Saudi government a conundrum, which they solved by allowing unmarried women to take paid positions in these boutiques as sales help. This was the only exception the Saudi government made to the ban on female employment.

Interestingly, the places within Islam that have made real progress toward women's equality are all American allies. The United Arab Emirates, Qatar, Kuwait and Iraq all allow women general rights in the areas of employment and, in the case of Kuwait and Iraq, the vote and the right to stand for office. This would not have taken place if not for the liberation of Kuwait and Iraq by force of American arms.

Finally, I want to discuss economic development and opportunity.

I know that for many, the face of globalization is contradictory. The Internet and television can bring knowledge and information, but also offensive sexuality and mindless violence. Trade can bring new wealth and opportunities, but also huge disruptions and changing communities. In all nations - including my own - this change can bring fear. Fear that because of modernity we will lose of control over our economic choices, our politics, and most importantly our identities - those things we most cherish about our communities, our families, our traditions, and our faith.

Indeed, the "offensive sexuality and mindless violence" objected to by Muslims, and many Christians and Jews, emerges from conflicts between free speech rights and community values — an unavoidable outcome of the First Amendment. Is Obama equating the resistance to change by Muslim and Christian conservatives? Is he suggesting that such resistance emerges from fear of change — one of the twin themes of his 2008 campaign?

But I also know that human progress cannot be denied. There need not be contradiction between development and tradition. Countries like Japan and South Korea grew their economies while maintaining distinct cultures. The same is true for the astonishing progress within Muslim-majority countries from Kuala Lumpur to Dubai. In ancient times and in our times, Muslim communities have been at the forefront of innovation and education.

"Countries like Japan and South Korea grew their economies enormously while maintaining distinct cultures." If you travel to East Asia today you are struck by the Westernization of Tokyo, Hong Kong, Singapore, and Seoul.

"In ancient times and in our times, Muslim communities have been at the forefront of innovation and education." Because of technological innovation the West caught up to Islam by 1500. By 1750, the West had far surpassed Muslim countries.

Center for Islamic Pluralism: "President Obama praised Dubai for its 'astonishing progress.' We would expect the American president to be aware that Dubai has suffered significantly in the current global economic crisis, and that its artificial prosperity is in danger."[72]

The progress of cities like Dubai comes from Western investment for the region's natural resources of oil. Oil was discovered in the region by British and American petroleum engineers around 1910, which was then developed in the 1920s and 1930s. After these resources had been tapped and developed by Westerners, the industry was nationalized. The region then diversified into electronics with Western capital.

The types of women's rights trumpeted by liberal Democrats do not exist in Islam. Abortion is strictly forbidden in Muslim countries. Muslims do not consider government funded birth control a universal right.[73] They do not consider the freedom of lesbians to marry and adopt children a great advance for civilization. The President does not recognize that the "rights" he considers universal for women do not exist in the Muslim world. Similarly, he refuses to admit that the rights of suffrage and office holding in the Muslim world have been guaranteed by the American military in wars he has openly criticized.

This is important because no development strategy can be based only upon what comes out of the ground, nor can it be sustained while young people are out of work. Many Gulf States have enjoyed great wealth as a consequence of oil, and some are beginning to focus it on broader development. But all of us must recognize that education and innovation will be the currency of the 21st century, and in too many Muslim communities there remains underinvestment in these areas. I am emphasizing such investments within my country. And while America in the past has focused on oil and gas in this part of the world, we now seek a broader engagement.

On education, we will expand exchange programs, and increase scholarships, like the one that brought my father to America, while encouraging more Americans to study in Muslim communities. And we will match promising Muslim students with internships in America; invest in on-line learning for teachers and children around the world; and create a new online network, so a teenager in Kansas can communicate instantly with a teenager in Cairo.

On economic development, we will create a new corps of business volunteers to partner with counterparts in Muslim-majority countries. And I will host a Summit on Entrepreneurship this year to identify how we can deepen ties between business leaders, foundations and social entrepreneurs in the United States and Muslim communities around the world.

"...I will hold a summit on entrepreneurship this year..." Obama has frequently been criticized for his lack of executive and business leadership experience. Obama went from law school to "community organizing," and then to running for public office. He has never had to meet a payroll. Many critics contend that he does not understand how tax policies affect small businesses. The American Action Forum, for example, in their report, note how Obama's calls to increase taxes on high earners create uncertainty for entrepreneurs, who are the engine to an economic recovery.[74] The two-day summit on entrepreneurship[75] for 50 mostly Muslim countries in April 2010 did not result in any substantive results. In fact, it came under criticism, with skeptics saying the main difficulties that entrepreneurs encounter in many Muslim-majority countries are the authoritarian and bureaucratic regimes governing them, which the summit did not address. Obama used his background as a community organizer to emphasize "social entrepreneurship,"[76] a concept quite different from real entrepreneurship.

Obama's business policies, while favoring big corporations who have the means to adhere to bureaucratic regulations (and indeed often help write them in their favor), are harming small businesses and entrepreneurs who find themselves at a disadvantage. Among the latest of his harmful policies has been the proposal to increase restrictions on S corporations on payroll tax exemptions. Blogger Moe Lane writes, "S-Corps are a common method by which small companies – mom-and-pop stores, individual professional workers, START-UP BUSINESSES – file their taxes."[77]

On science and technology, we will launch a new fund to support technological development in Muslim-majority countries, and to help transfer ideas to the marketplace so they can create jobs. We will open centers of scientific excellence in Africa, the Middle East and Southeast Asia, and appoint new Science Envoys to collaborate on programs that develop new sources of energy, create green jobs, digitize records, clean water, and grow new crops. And today I am announcing a new global effort with the Organization of the Islamic Conference to eradicate polio. And we will also expand partnerships with Muslim communities to promote child and maternal health.

All these things must be done in partnership. Americans are ready to join with citizens and governments; community organizations, religious leaders, and businesses in Muslim communities around the world to help our people pursue a better life.

The issues that I have described will not be easy to address. But we have a responsibility to join together on behalf of the world we seek - a world where extremists no longer threaten our people, and American troops have come home; a world where Israelis and Palestinians are each secure in a state of their own, and nuclear energy is used for peaceful purposes; a world where governments serve their citizens, and the rights of all God's children are respected. Those are mutual interests. That is the world we seek. But we can only achieve it together.

This forward-looking vision of a peaceful world provides encouragement and a sense of shared goals — appropriate for such a political speech. Obama gives listeners the benefit of the doubt in assuming "mutual interests."

I know there are many - Muslim and non-Muslim - who question whether we can forge this new beginning. Some are eager to stoke the flames of division, and to stand in the way of progress. Some suggest that it isn't worth the effort - that we are fated to disagree, and civilizations are doomed to clash. Many more are simply skeptical that real change can occur. There is so much fear, so much mistrust. But if we choose to be bound by the past, we will never move forward. And I want to particularly say this to young people of every faith, in every country - you, more than anyone, have the ability to remake this world.

"...to young people of every faith, in every country-you, more than anyone, have the ability to reimagine the world, to remake the world." This statement recalls the 2008 rallying cry, "Yes We Can!" But is "remaking the world" realistic — especially through a "reimagining"? Obama is appealing to the perennial conceit of youth and that is the ability to improve upon their elders, in ways never before imaginable, to the point of remaking the world. Ultimately, such a transformation requires a transformation of human nature. When resistance by ordinary people arrives, revolutionaries taken up with their utopian beliefs go to extraordinary means to force conversion. For example, peasant farmers resisted Soviet agricultural collectivism (part of the transformation of the economic system) by destroying crops and putting their own lives at risk in opposition. The twentieth century, particularly, is filled with the millions of bodies sacrificed for the unrealistic dreams of revolutionaries.

All of us share this world for but a brief moment in time. The question is whether we spend that time focused on what pushes us apart, or whether we commit ourselves to an effort - a sustained effort - to find common ground, to focus on the future we seek for our children, and to respect the dignity of all human beings.

Here, Obama, in referring to "common ground," is appealing to ethos—a laudable effort. Aristotle lists three ways to appeal to audiences: ethos, pathos, and logos. Logos is logical appeal; pathos is emotional appeal. Ethos refers to the speaker's or writer's character--in the words of Aristotle, "Persuasion is achieved by the speaker's personal character when the speech is so spoken as to make us think him credible" (Book 1, Chapter 2 of *The Rhetoric*). Obama, by illustrating what he and his audience have in common is establishing the fact that he is someone of goodwill. See Aristotle and Crider for more details.

It is easier to start wars than to end them. It is easier to blame others than to look inward; to see what is different about someone than to find the things we share. But we should choose the right path, not just the easy path. There is also one rule that lies at the heart of every religion - that we do unto others as we would have them do unto us. This truth transcends nations and peoples - a belief that isn't new; that isn't black or white or brown; that isn't Christian, or Muslim or Jew. It's a belief that pulsed in the cradle of civilization, and that still beats in the heart of billions. It's a faith in other people, and it's what brought me here today.

"one rule that lies at the heart of every religion-that we do unto others as we would have them do unto us." The Golden Rule is a Christian truth. There is no equivalent in Islam: "Islam enjoins treating other Muslims well, NOT those of other religions—unlike Jesus who said to treat 'others'—not just other Jews (or Christians) well."[78]

We have the power to make the world we seek, but only if we have the courage to make a new beginning, keeping in mind what has been written.

The Holy Koran tells us, "O mankind! We have created you male and a female; and we have made you into nations and tribes so that you may know one another."

The Talmud tells us: "The whole of the Torah is for the purpose of promoting peace."

The Holy Bible tells us, "Blessed are the peacemakers, for they shall be called sons of God."

"The Holy Bible tells us: 'Blessed are the peacemakers, for they shall be called sons of God.'" Obama quotes the Bible very late in the speech.

The people of the world can live together in peace. We know that is God's vision. Now, that must be our work here on Earth. Thank you. And may God's peace be upon you.

"...And may god's peace be upon you." He signed off with the Muslim farewell, without using the Hebrew "shalom," or the Christian invocation, "Good night and God bless you."

Center for Islamic Pluralism again: "As Muslims, we consider such rhetorical trimmings by a non-Muslim speaker to be superfluous and ignorant. Muslims do not expect non-Muslims like President Obama to say 'assalaamu alaykum,' to praise Qur'an in an Islamic idiom, or to add the phrase 'peace be upon them' in speaking about God's prophets. These are artifacts of our religion. For non-Muslims to use them is gratuitous and pretentious, and appears bizarre -- as strange as it would be to hear a Muslim cleric refer to God by the Hebrew phrase 'baruch Hashem' (blessed be the creator) or say 'Jesus is Lord.'"[79]

Chapter 6

"A New Beginning" in the Historical Context of American Foreign Policy

When a student or an observer delves into this topic more deeply he sees that Obama is projecting a major break with one American tradition, while aligning himself with another one. Are the American people necessarily receptive to calls to "remake the world?" Do people warm to such grandiloquent rhetoric, only to lose interest when they find that remaking the world may not be so easy after all? Furthermore, once the world is remade, then what is the next step? A cursory look at the American historical past, particularly our foreign policy tradition, is in order here.

American foreign policy developed gradually over time. As a nation we generally adhered to Washington's maxim on avoiding foreign entanglements when possible. The first three Presidents resisted involving America in foreign wars, and the fourth President, James Madison, asked for a declaration of war against Britain, only after repeated provocations and aggression. The War of 1812 ended in a draw, but America teetered on the brink of disaster numerous times in the conflict. The British raided freely along the American coast, they sacked Washington D.C. in 1814, and the war strained the American economy to the breaking point, virtually wrecking the financial system. The 1812-15 experience convinced many public figures that war was an unpredictable crucible, best avoided, if possible.

The first American statement of foreign policy was the celebrated Monroe Doctrine note, issued in December of 1823. The Monroe Doctrine was largely the work of John Quincy Adams, the Secretary of State in the Monroe Administration.

In the doctrine the USA pledged to stop the feared re-colonization of Latin America by Spain, and stated that the Americas were no longer to be considered sources of colonization. This was a message sent to Spain, Portugal, France, Russia and to a lesser extent Britain, putting them on notice that efforts to extend colonialism in the Western Hemisphere would be considered as deliberately unfriendly to the United States. The doctrine did not commit the country to war, although it left open that possibility.

Interestingly, the Monroe Doctrine also set out the standard for a future American approach to the question of empires, colonies, and freedom seeking revolutions. We pledged, in the Doctrine, that we would not interfere in areas that were already parts of an imperial system. We sought to assure the British that we had no designs on Canada, we wanted the Spanish to understand that we did not intend to invade Cuba and considered Alaska to be Russian territory. Those areas were colonies of foreign powers and we did not intend to alter the balance of power. Finally, Adams addressed the question of America as the revolutionary vanguard nation. He stated flatly that we did not sally forth looking for giants to slay. America, Adams stated, was the friend of liberty everywhere, but the guarantor only of our own.

The United States generally adhered to the doctrine as our foreign policy guide throughout the nineteenth century. We did not intervene in civil wars in places like Hungary and Poland and we did not officially support independence movements in places like Cuba or Ireland. While few foreign nations accepted the Monroe Doctrine as a legitimate and binding statement, they tended to avoid provoking the United States as the country grew richer and stronger. We did fight a war against Mexico in 1846-48, and in a jingoistic fit we thrashed Spain in 1898, but the nation basically tried to sidestep international entanglements until 1917.

The first major change in the entire theme underpinning American foreign policy came with the American declaration of war against Germany in 1917. The First World War had broken out in the summer of 1914, and the USA declared its neutrality on August 4th. Over the next two years the warring sides tried to appease the United States or to actively bring her into the war. Generally the German coalition, known as the Central Powers, applied the former strategy, while the British coalition, known as the Allies, pursued the latter approach.

But Germany saw no way out of the deadlock on the Western Front after 1917, except by opting for unrestricted submarine warfare against Britain. After a series of aggressive German actions involving submarine attacks on merchant and passenger ships, American public opinion swung sharply against Germany by the fall of 1916. The Germans announced that they would begin attacking civilian shipping without restrictions on February 1, 1917, and, later in the month, American operatives uncovered a German plot to use Mexico as a surrogate to attack the United States. The Congress declared war on Germany on April 6, 1917.

President Woodrow Wilson listed these German offenses in his war message to Congress, but did not emphasize these as the primary reason for his decision to ask for authority to begin war with Germany. He stated, in a rhetorical flourish, that we were going to war, "to make the world safe for democracy" even though our Russian allies did not practice democracy, and our British allies refused to allow this for their subject peoples. The traditional understanding of the nature of foreign policy was that a successful foreign policy advanced the interests of the United States. Wilson upped the ante here, and substituted the promotion of worldwide democracy as the ultimate goal of American foreign policy.

The First World War was generally very popular with the American public. The nation put over 5,000,000 men under arms, and American manpower provided the necessary strength to break the back of the last German offensive in the summer of 1918. Revolution broke out in Germany in late October, Kaiser Wilhelm II slipped off into exile on November

9, 1918, and the Germans surrendered on November 11, 1918. The result seemed to vindicate Wilson's ideas and he played the role of conquering hero, wise lawgiver, and savior of the world with great relish. However, a look beneath the surface revealed trouble ahead.

The American people wanted to punish Germany for aggressive actions and designs. They were much less enthusiastic about "making the world safe for democracy." Despite Wilson's personal pleas the public issued the President's Democratic Party a severe defeat in the midterm elections of November 5, 1918. The euphoria that greeted the German surrender the following week masked the fact that 116,000 American servicemen had fallen during the war. Wilson suffered the indignity of watching the US Senate reject the peace treaty he had personally negotiated at the close of the war. The American people soundly rejected the idea of making the world safe for democracy.

The reaction against what has become known as "Liberal Internationalism" began as the First World War wound down and continued for the next twenty years. The beginning of another great war in Europe on September 1, 1939, brought no strong surge of internationalist feeling among the American people. On the contrary the German invasion of Poland and the spread of the war simply spawned a desire on the part of the people to stay out of the conflict. This attitude changed only after the Japanese sneak attack on Pearl Harbor on December 7, 1941, the declaration of war on Japan the following day, and the German and Italian declarations of war on the United States on December 11th.

President John F. Kennedy most closely resembles Obama in his youth, his telegenic qualities, his surface eloquence and his idealistic call to youth to remake the world. As mentioned earlier, Kennedy confidently pledged his people to go anywhere, bear any burden, and fight any foe, etc. to ensure the survival of liberty in the world. This soaring rhetoric lit a fire in the minds of many idealistic college-age students in

America at that time. Did these students actually understand what the President meant? Did they actually respond to his call?

American college students of the 1960s claimed to love JFK, and his memory still holds a certain reverence for people of that generation. A close look at the evidence, however, proves that few actually practiced what Kennedy preached. The JFK mission crashed on the shoals of Vietnam. The war divided the nation like no other issue since slavery, and young people, many who proclaimed their love of Kennedy, refused induction to the military to fight for this ideal. They would not "go anywhere, pay any price," etc., and the grand call to remake the world fell apart in a few short years.

The American people tend to love high-sounding rhetoric, and to respond favorably to calls to change the world, but only for a short period of time. We generally do not like the follow through, and the messy business of getting these plans off of the drawing board, and into practice. When all is said and done, most Americans prefer to take care of business at home, instead of setting off on foreign adventures.

Obama's call for a new and open relationship between America and Islam may well crash on the treacherous shoals of Muslim extremism. The grand hopes of the "Arab Spring" of 2011 are now fading as Westerners see the emergence of governments led by the Muslim Brotherhood in Egypt and Libya, and renewed extremist activity in Yemen, Saudi Arabia, and the United Arab Emirates.

Selected Bibliography

1. JM Roberts, *The New Penguin History of the World* (1997), is a good general world history, and is strong on Islam.

2. Stanley Elkins and Erik McKitrick, *The Age of Federalism* (1993), is the best single volume history on Washington's Presidency, and the Farewell Address.

3. Norman Graebner, *Ideas And Diplomacy: Readings in the Intellectual Tradition of the American Foreign Policy* (2000), is a good recent work on foreign policy and is quite strong concerning the Monroe Doctrine.

4. The literature on Woodrow Wilson is vast. The standard work is: *Arthur S. Link, Woodrow Wilson: Revolution, War, And Peace* (1979). For a recent and critical view of Wilson see Thomas Fleming, *The Illusion of Victory: America in World War I* (2003).

5. For John F. Kennedy and the crisis of his times, *Grand Expectations: The United States 1945-1974* by James Patterson (1996) provides a good overview.

Chapter 7

The Results: What Has Happened Since the Speech

Much has happened in the last three years in the Middle East. While some herald the "Arab Spring" as a promise of democracy in the region, others see ominous signs.

Obama was unable to fulfill many of his campaign promises, like closing Guantanamo. In fact, much of his rhetoric has not differed much from President Bush's, a fact noted with irony by the right and with anger by the left. Yet, the protests against the war — so frequent during the Bush administration — have all but disappeared.

In that same spring, a Pew poll showed that since the Cairo speech Obama and the United States have suffered a decline in favorable opinion among most of the Middle Eastern nations, especially in Turkey and the Palestinian countries, as well as Indonesia.[80] In terms of the Palestinian conflict the *Washington Post* in a July 14, 2012, analysis, concluded that Obama's "tough talk" on Israel and "A New Beginning" speech failed to bring about a peace deal and alienated Israel.[81]

While soldiers still die in Afghanistan, Obama has changed the strategy of warfare, by relying more on drone attacks, executed under his direction. Obama makes the final decision regarding strikes, making judgment calls when drone attacks might kill innocent bystanders. These actions are recorded as "without precedent in presidential history" in a lengthy *New York Times* article on Obama's "secret kill list."[82] (Such revelations brought bipartisan calls for investigations on whether these were deliberate White House leaks that compromised national security for the purpose of advancing Obama's reelection.)[83]

In their editorial, "Too Much Power for a President," on May 31, 2012, the *Times* editors wrote, "No one in [the president's] position should be able to unilaterally order the killing of American citizens or foreigners located far from a battlefield— depriving Americans of their due process rights—without the consent of someone outside his political inner circle."[84]

Columnist Charles Krauthammer noted that Obama's take-no-prisoners approach, while obviating the need for holding terrorist suspects (as in Guantanamo), yields no intelligence.[85] In a highly critical article, *Foreign Policy* writer, Jonathan Turley, listed the ways that the new policy, outlined by Attorney General Eric Holder in a speech, violated the principles of the founding of this country and eliminated due process.[86] The American Civil Liberties Union also filed a lawsuit to obtain information about the targeted killing program, objecting that "few things are as dangerous to American liberty as the proposition that the government should be able to kill citizens anywhere in the world" without evidence being submitted to a court.[87] Such unprecedented acts of power by the president are being objected to by activists on both the right and left.

Clearly, much has happened in the interim between President Obama's speech in 2009 and when this guide went to press in the summer of 2012, as his second presidential campaign got into full swing. When the editors of the *Norton Reader* decided to include the speech in the textbook they had no way of knowing how his presidency would turn out. They had no way of knowing what his vision of "remaking the world" would turn out to be. Yet, in one of the topic questions, they decided to ask students how they would follow his lead in this respect. The assumption embedded in the question is that students should heed this call, regardless.[88]

The fact that the outcome of Obama's promises and presidency was not known and tested should have given pause to the editors of the textbooks. Sadly, however, the inclusion of this speech evidences the decay of academic standards as more and more professors see themselves as activists in the classroom. But we hope that this guide provided a bit of insight and historical context.

It is up to your generation to call out such professors for their biases and errors. We believe that speaking up in this way will not only benefit the cause of education reform, but also the development of your skills in writing and argumentation, as well as character. If you see such assignments as challenges and are willing to do the extra research, you will make yourself a better writer and debater. That certainly is the preferred alternative to simply echoing a teacher's political ideology.

Chapter 8

How to Answer the Assignment Questions Without Jeopardizing Your Grade

Following are the questions that appear in the *Norton Reader*. Such questions with built-in biases too frequently fill the pages of many current textbooks. You can apply the strategies discussed here to similarly framed questions in other textbooks, on other topics.

To protect yourself, remember to keep copies of your papers in case you need to challenge your teacher's or professor's grade. You should not be punished for challenging a professor who imposes his political views on students. If you are, challenge the grade by taking it up through the appropriate channels in your school. Your student handbook should tell how to do this.

When writing or debating, always be fair and logical, and provide ample support. Make sure your paper is free of errors and clearly written and organized. Professors will be less likely to punish students for not agreeing with their biases if they know that students will not be intimidated and can make logical, clear, and well-supported arguments. You can start that trend, help future students, and do your part to help reform education!

THE TOPIC QUESTIONS

1.) Obama begins his speech with a long introduction that is simultaneously political, historical, and personal. How does the introduction prepare for the discussion of specific issues that follow?

I am honored to be in the timeless city of Cairo, and to be hosted by two remarkable institutions. For over a thousand years, Al-Azhar has stood as a beacon of Islamic learning, and for over a century, Cairo University has been a source of Egypt's advancement. Together, you represent the harmony between tradition and progress. I am grateful for your hospitality, and the hospitality of the people of Egypt. I am also proud to carry with me the goodwill of the American people, and a greeting of peace from Muslim communities in my country: assalaamu alaykum.

In traditional rhetorical practice, Obama here graciously compliments his hosts and his audience, and thanks them for their hospitality. As elected leader, he is right to extend greetings of goodwill from the American people. But as noted earlier, some American Muslims were offended by his inappropriate use of the Muslim greeting. He might be a bit presumptuous to speak for "Muslim communities in my country" — especially given his repeated claims to be a Christian, and not a Muslim. See earlier pages for discussion of this part of the speech.

We meet at a time of tension between the United States and Muslims around the world - tension rooted in historical forces that go beyond any current policy debate. The relationship between Islam and the West includes centuries of co-existence and cooperation, but also conflict and religious wars. More recently, tension has been fed by colonialism that denied rights and opportunities to many Muslims, and a Cold War in which Muslim-majority countries were too often treated as proxies without regard to their own aspirations. Moreover, the sweeping change brought by modernity and globalization led many Muslims to view the West as hostile to the traditions of Islam.

See earlier pages for discussion about the historical misrepresentation of colonialism. While it is certainly appropriate for a political leader to focus on the nice things about his hosts and listeners, and therefore build his own credibility, it is another thing for an American president to present such a skewed picture of history that presents his own country and traditions in a falsely negative light. After all, a

leader of a country should first be proud of his own country —
not besmirch it, especially on foreign soil.

*Violent extremists have exploited these tensions in a small but
potent minority of Muslims. The attacks of September 11th, 2001
and the continued efforts of these extremists to engage in violence
against civilians has led some in my country to view Islam as
inevitably hostile not only to America and Western countries, but
also to human rights. This has bred more fear and mistrust.*

Obama presents the sins of the West (colonialism) as inherent
parts of the culture's overall make-up. He implies that it was
all of Western culture that took part in colonialism. So the sin
of colonialism was a sin of the West. In contrast, here he is
careful to point to "a small but potent minority of Muslims."
So, while colonialism is presented as a defining feature of the
West, terrorism is not of the East, or Islam.

*So long as our relationship is defined by our differences, we will
empower those who sow hatred rather than peace, and who promote
conflict rather than the cooperation that can help all of our people
achieve justice and prosperity. This cycle of suspicion and discord
must end.*

Many political leaders call for unity and do it by invoking
common goals, like "justice and prosperity." But one must
ask: did Obama go beyond presidential graciousness to
prostrating his own country and people before a foreign
power? Was this part of the "blame America" strategy (his
apology tour) that angered so many Americans?

As the editors of the textbook imply, the introduction does
"prepare for the discussions of specific issues that follow."
These specific issues include tensions between Muslim
countries and the United States. But the ground is laid by
casting more blame on one side. The solutions then involve
addressing the misdeeds of the U.S.

(The issues are handled in the earlier pages that explicate the
speech.)

2.) In the body of his speech, Obama discusses seven specific tensions or issues affecting the current relationship between the United States and Muslim nations. Select one of these sections and examine it in detail. How does Obama develop his argument so that it will appeal to various audiences?

The first part of the topic can be addressed by reviewing the analysis in the earlier part of the guide.

The second part, however, has the answer embedded within the question. Notice, the question is not "*Does* Obama appeal to various audiences?" Clearly, many felt that he appealed mostly to Muslim foreigners and those holding anti-American sentiments. While he does acknowledge the good of America, these acknowledgements were outnumbered by those that blamed America. You should closely examine wording around the topic you choose, as well as the overall appeals.

3.) Compare the introduction and the conclusion. How does Obama's stance toward the relationship between Americans and Muslims change from the beginning to the end of the speech?

Again, the answer is embedded in the question, "How does Obama's stance . . . change?" Does it change? That certainly is a fair question and one that you as a student should investigate before you accept the editors' assumptions. Could an argument be made that Obama's stance is consistent from beginning to end? While Obama does, as to be expected of someone giving a political speech, call for action at the end, can we say his stance changes? He does add a short quotation from the New Testament, but that is the only reference to Christianity in a supposedly ecumenical address. Is Western religion and culture still obscured? Re-read the speech carefully. Catalogue and count the references. The way to make your case is with support.

4.) Obama concludes with a call to action directed especially toward the world's youth: "And I want to particularly say this to young people of every faith, in every country — you more than anyone, have the ability to reimagine the world, to remake this world" (paragraph 68). Write a paper in which you discuss ways you personally might respond to this call.

Again, the answer is embedded in the topic. You are asked to discuss ways you might respond to this call. It is implied that you *should* heed Obama's call. But why? You are under no obligation to follow any political position or follow any political orders — especially in a class where you are presumably learning how to write informed, argumentative papers. Although the option of rejecting this call is not offered, it does not mean you should not take it upon yourself to do so. Turn the topic around. Research the history of radical movements, like the French Revolution and the Russian Revolution, both revolutions that began with the impulse to not only reform political regimes, but to remake the world, beginning with religion, customs, familial relationships, and social mores, not to mention economic and political systems. Such efforts resulted in dictatorial and totalitarian regimes.

And like John F. Kennedy, Obama appealed to the youth of our nation. While the youth are less inclined to be bound and restricted by habit and tradition, they also have less experience and knowledge. That is why radical transformations are almost always instigated by the young, particularly those in college, where such ideas incubate. That is why radicals target the young and often choose teaching as a profession. In contrast, the Founding Fathers looked to history and the traditions of the British political system. Their prudence has given us the longest-lasting Constitution in history, peaceful transitions of leadership, freedom, and prosperity.

[1] http://www.mindingthecampus.com/originals/2012/03/the_terrible_textbooks_of_freshman_comp.html

[2] http://www.youtube.com/watch?v=5AEEee8kCG4&feature=related

[3] http://www.youtube.com/watch?v=TW9b0xr06qA

[4] http://www.youtube.com/watch?v=wOtGr1JFCnE

[5] http://www.eagleforum.org/publications/educate/may12/middle-schoolers-drafted.html

[6] http://realdebatewisconsin.blogspot.com/2008/10/racine-schools-hand-out-textbook-with.html

[7] http://articles.cnn.com/2009-09-04/politics/obama.schools_1_obama-school-speech-policy-speech-white-house?_s=PM:POLITICS

[8] http://pewresearch.org/pubs/1031/young-voters-in-the-2008-election

[9] Two articles from rhetoric journals are representative. In "One Dream: Barack Obama, Race, and the American Dream" (*Rhetoric & Public Affairs*, Vol. 14, No.1, 2011), professors Robert C. Rowland and John M. Jones conclude that Obama in his speech on race and Rev. Jeremiah Wright "did more than read a teleprompter; he read the feelings of millions of his fellow citizens and pointed them toward a better future, a more perfect union." Jason Thompson, conversely, compared George W. Bush's rhetoric to Adolf Hitler's in "Magic for a People Trained in Pragmatism: Kenneth Burke, Mein Kampf, and the Early 9/11 Oratory of George W. Bush" (*Rhetoric Review*, September 2011)

[10] http://www.mindingthecampus.com/originals/2011/04/_after_spending_four.html

11http://dailycaller.com/2012/04/10/obama-admirer-to-teach-understanding-obama-class-at-harvard-law-school/

12 http://keywiki.org/index.php/Charles_Ogletree#cite_note-7

13http://www.itsabouttimebpp.com/Announcements/Former_Black_Panthers.html

14http://www.law.harvard.edu/academics/curriculum/catalog/index.html?o=64810

15http://www.cbsnews.com/8301-503544_162-5063097-503544.html

16http://www.guardian.co.uk/commentisfree/2009/jun/05/barack-obama-speech-cairo

17http://www.nytimes.com/2009/06/05/opinion/05fri1.html?_r=2

18http://blog.heritage.org/2009/06/03/morning-bell-president-obamas-top-ten-apologies/

19http://www.nytimes.com/2009/06/05/opinion/05fri1.html?_r=1

20http://www.washingtontimes.com/news/2009/jun/5/obama-gives-a-bush-speech/print/

21http://www.nationalreview.com/articles/227651/obama-cairo-now-what/editors

22http://www.washingtontimes.com/news/2009/jun/5/obama-gives-a-bush-speech/

23http://www.islamicpluralism.org/1464/muslims-oin-obama-in-cairo

24 Cicero, *On Oratory and Orators*. Translated or Edited, J.S. Watson. Southern Illinois University Press; Carbondale and Edwardsville. 1970. xx.

[25] Ibid. 10-11.

[26] In addition to the two editions of Aristotle and Cicero, we suggest *The Office of Assertion: An Art of Rhetoric* for the Academic Essay, by Scott Crider (2005, ISI Books).

[27] http://gwpapers.virginia.edu/documents/farewell/transcript.html

[28] http://gwpapers.virginia.edu/documents/farewell/intro.html

[29] http://www.fordham.edu/halsall/mod/1865lincoln-aug2.asp

[30] http://www.presidency.ucsb.edu/ws/index.php?pid=8032#axzz1sgoE2oW7

[31] This group would have been 25 to 45 years old — a bit older than the cohort candidates appeal to now when they attempt to capture the youth vote, those who are eager to implement new ideas. But the generation Kennedy was referring to had grown up during the Great Depression and fought in World War II; they were the "Greatest Generation" by current parlance. The voting age in 1961 was still 21.

[32] http://www.islamicpluralism.org/1464/muslims-oin-obama-in-cairo

[33] *Ibid.*

[34] *Ibid.*

[35] Slann, Martin. "Democracy and Totalitarian Islam: The Definitional Framework for World War IV." Florida Political Science Association, March 2010.

[36] http://www.nationalreview.com/articles/299782/western-sharia-andrew-c-mccarthy?pg=1

[37] http://pjmedia.com/blog/islamist-perfidy-and-western-naivety-which-is-more-lethal/

38http://www.islamicpluralism.org/1464/muslims-oin-obama-in-cairo

39 http://victorhanson.com/articles/hanson121909.html

40http://www.islamicpluralism.org/1464/muslims-oin-obama-in-cairo

41 http://victorhanson.com/articles/hanson121909.html

42 This is true, but Morocco's recognition, that beat the French by a month, didn't carry much weight. The recognition came not from support of republican principles that American independence represented, but from what Morocco perceived as the U.S.'s vulnerability once she had lost the protection of the British Empire.

43 http://hnn.us/articles/91942.html

44 Dr. Timothy Furnish recommends *Power, Faith and Fantasy: America in the Middle East, 1776 to the Present* by Michael Oren (W.W. Norton, 2007).

45http://www.powerlineblog.com/archives/2007/07/017881.php

46http://www.powerlineblog.com/archives/2006/11/015621.php

47 http://keywiki.org/index.php/Keith_Ellison

48 http://www.humanevents.com/article.php?id=40141

49 http://www.nationalreview.com/articles/227651/obama-cairo-now-what/editors

50 Slann, Ibid.

51http://www.islamicpluralism.org/1464/muslims-oin-obama-in-cairo

52 Slann, Ibid. page 14.

53 http://www.nationalreview.com/articles/227651/obama-cairo-now-what/editors

54http://www.washingtontimes.com/news/2009/jun/5/obama-gives-a-bush-speech/print/

55 National Association of Scholars lecture, Emory University, October 6, 2010. See McCarthy, *The Grand Jihad: How Islam and the Left Sabotage America*. Encounter Books, 2010.

56http://uscpublicdiplomacy.org/index.php/newswire/cpdblog_detail/jefferson_on_soft_power_behind_obamas_cairo_quote/

57http://www.guardian.co.uk/world/2003/mar/20/iraq.georgebush

58 http://www.commondreams.org/headlines03/0907-10.htm

59 http://aei.org/article/foreign-and-defense-policy/regional/middle-east-and-north-africa/be-warned-americas-withdrawal-from-iraq-heralds-a-world-of-instability/60

60http://online.wsj.com/article/SB10001424052702304363104577390141194301150.html

61 Slann, Ibid., page 10.

62 Slann, Ibid. page 5.

63http://www.islamicpluralism.org/1464/muslims-oin-obama-in-cairo

64 Kamrava, Mehran. *The Political History of Modern Iran: From Tribalism to Theocracy*. Praeger; Westport, Connecticut, 1992. 58-67.

65 http://victorhanson.com/articles/hanson121909.html

66 *The New Penguin History of the World*, London; Penguin Books, 2002. 330-331.

67 http://victorhanson.com/articles/hanson121909.html

68http://www.islamicpluralism.org/1464/muslims-oin-obama-in-cairo

69 Email from Furnish to Mary Grabar, May 23, 2012.

70 http://www.missionislam.com/knowledge/zakat.htm

71http://www.newenglishreview.org/Jerry_Gordon/Zakat_and_Terrorism/

72http://www.islamicpluralism.org/1464/muslims-oin-obama-in-cairo

73 The 2012 case of Sandra Fluke who testified for federal health care to provide her with contraceptives is summarized here http://en.wikipedia.org/wiki/Rush_Limbaugh%E2%80%93Sandra_Fluke_controversy

74http://americanactionforum.org/sites/default/files/Future_of_Taxes_and_Small_Biz_final%5B1%5D.pdf

75http://www.pbs.org/newshour/rundown/2010/04/entrepreneurship-summit.html

76 http://www.csmonitor.com/USA/Politics/2010/0426/At-summit-on-entrepreneurship-Obama-s-approach-to-Muslim-world-on-display

77http://www.redstate.com/moe_lane/2012/04/25/president-obama-encouragingplanning-to-tax-into-oblivion-start-up-businesses/

78 Furnish, Tim. Email correspondence May 23, 2012.

79http://www.islamicpluralism.org/1464/muslims-oin-obama-in-cairo

80 http://www.pewglobal.org/2011/05/17/chapter-1-opinions-of-the-u-s-and-president-barack-obama/

[81]http://www.washingtonpost.com/politics/obama-searches-for-middle-east-peace/2012/07/14/gJQAQQiKlW_story.html?wpisrc=nl_headlines

[82]http://www.nytimes.com/2012/05/29/world/obamas-leadership-in-war-on-al-qaeda.html?ref=sunday

[83]http://www.washingtonpost.com/politics/senate-republicans-call-for-special-prosecutor-in-white-house-leaks-probe/2012/06/12/gJQA5KoxXV_story.html

[84] http://www.nytimes.com/2012/05/31/opinion/too-much-power-for-a-president.html?ref=world#h[]

[85]http://mdjonline.com/view/full_story/18821222/article-Barack-Obama--Drone-Warrior?instance=special%20_coverage_right_column

[86]http://www.foreignpolicy.com/articles/2012/03/06/obama_s_kill_doctrine

[87] http://www.aclu.org/national-security/aclu-comment-eric-holder-speech-targeted-killing-program

[88] See section below for tips on answering such questions.

Made in the USA
Charleston, SC
21 October 2012